MznLnx

Missing Links Exam Preps

Exam Prep for

Management: Challenges for Tomorrow's Leaders

Lewis, Goodman, Fandt, & Michlitsch, 5th Edition

The MznLnx Exam Prep is your link from the texbook and lecture to your exams.
The MznLnx Exam Preps are unauthorized and comprehensive reviews of your textbooks.

All material provided by MznLnx and Rico Publications (c) 2010
Textbook publishers and textbook authors do not particpate in or contribute to these reviews.

MznLnx

Rico
Publications

Exam Prep for Management: Challenges for Tomorrow's Leaders
5th Edition
Lewis, Goodman, Fandt, & Michlitsch

Publisher: Raymond Houge
Assistant Editor: Michael Rouger
Text and Cover Designer: Lisa Buckner
Marketing Manager: Sara Swagger
Project Manager, Editorial Production: Jerry Emerson
Art Director: Vernon Lowerui

Product Manager: Dave Mason
Editorial Asitant: Rachel Guzmanji
Pedagogy: Debra Long
Cover Image: Jim Reed/Getty Images
Text and Cover Printer: City Printing, Inc.
Compositor: Media Mix, Inc.

(c) 2010 Rico Publications
ALL RIGHTS RESERVED. No part of this work
covered by the copyright may be reproduced or
used in any form or by an means--graphic, electronic,
or mechanical, including photocopying, recording,
taping, Web distribution, information storage, and
retrieval systems, or in any other manner--without the
written permission of the publisher.

Printed in the United States
ISBN:

For more information about our products, contact us at:
Dave.Mason@RicoPublications.com

For permission to use material from this text or
product, submit a request online to:
Dave.Mason@RicoPublications.com

Contents

CHAPTER 1
Management and Managers — 1

CHAPTER 2
Evolution of Management Thought — 6

CHAPTER 3
Social Responsibility and Ethics — 13

CHAPTER 4
Strategic Management and Planning in a Global Environment — 17

CHAPTER 5
Planning in the Contemporary Organization — 24

CHAPTER 6
Managerial Decision Making — 30

CHAPTER 7
Organizing for Effectiveness and Efficiency — 36

CHAPTER 8
Organizational Design — 40

CHAPTER 9
Strategic Human Resource Management — 43

CHAPTER 10
Organizational Culture and Change — 53

CHAPTER 11
Communicating Effectively within Diverse Organizations — 54

CHAPTER 12
Leading in a Dynamic Environment — 55

CHAPTER 13
Exploring Individual Differences and Team Dynamics — 58

CHAPTER 14
Motivating Organizational Members — 63

CHAPTER 15
Organizational Control in a Complex Business Environment — 67

CHAPTER 16
Productivity and Quality in Operations — 72

CHAPTER 17
Information Technology and Control — 80

ANSWER KEY — 84

TO THE STUDENT

COMPREHENSIVE

The *MznLnx* Exam Prep series is designed to help you pass your exams. Editors at MznLnx review your textbooks and then prepare these practice exams to help you master the textbook material. Unlike study guides, workbooks, and practice tests provided by the texbook publisher and textbook authors, *MznLnx* gives you **all** of the material in each chapter in exam form, not just samples, so you can be sure to nail your exam.

MECHANICAL

The MznLnx Exam Prep series creates exams that will help you learn the subject matter as well as test you on your understanding. Each question is designed to help you master the concept. Just working through the exams, you gain an understanding of the subject--its a simple mechanical process that produces success.

INTEGRATED STUDY GUIDE AND REVIEW

MznLnx is not just a set of exams designed to test you, its also a comprehensive review of the subject content. Each exam question is also a review of the concept, making sure that you will get the answer correct without having to go to other sources of material. You learn as you go! Its the easiest way to pass an exam.

HUMOR

Studying can be tedious and dry. MznLnx's instructional design includes moderate humor within the exam questions on occassion, to break the tedium and revitalize the brain

Chapter 1. Management and Managers

1. A _____ is a list of the general tasks and responsibilities of a position. Typically, it also includes to whom the position reports, specifications such as the qualifications needed by the person in the job, salary range for the position, etc. A _____ is usually developed by conducting a job analysis, which includes examining the tasks and sequences of tasks necessary to perform the job.

    a. Recruitment advertising
    b. Recruitment
    c. Job description
    d. Recruitment Process Insourcing

2. In politics, a _____, (by metaphor with the carved _____ at the prow of a sailing ship), is a person who holds an important title or office yet executes little actual power, most commonly limited by convention rather than law. Common _____s include constitutional monarchs, such as: Queen Elizabeth II, the Emperor of Japan, or presidents in parliamentary democracies, such as the President of Israel.

    While the authority of a _____ is in practice generally symbolic, public opinion, respect for the office or the office holder and access to high levels of government can give them significant influence on events.

    a. Figurehead
    b. 33 Strategies of War
    c. 28-hour day
    d. 1990 Clean Air Act

3. _____ has been described as the 'process of social influence in which one person can enlist the aid and support of others in the accomplishment of a common task' . A definition more inclusive of followers comes from Alan Keith of Genentech who said '_____ is ultimately about creating a way for people to contribute to making something extraordinary happen.'

    _____ is one of the most salient aspects of the organizational context. However, defining _____ has been challenging.

    a. 28-hour day
    b. 1990 Clean Air Act
    c. Situational leadership
    d. Leadership

4. An _____ is a person who has possession of an enterprise and assumes significant accountability for the inherent risks and the outcome. It is an ambitious leader who combines land, labor, and capital to create and market new goods or services. The term is a loanword from French and was first defined by the Irish economist Richard Cantillon.

a. A Stake in the Outcome
b. Entrepreneur
c. AAAI
d. A4e

5. _____ is used to assign the available resources in an economic way. It is part of resource management.

In strategic planning,is a plan for using available resources, for example human resources, especially in the near term, to achieve goals for the future.

a. 33 Strategies of War
b. 1990 Clean Air Act
c. 28-hour day
d. Resource allocation

6. _____ for short is a descriptive term for certain executives in a business operation. It is also a formal title held by some business executives, most commonly in the hospitality industry.

A _____ has broad, overall responsibility for a business or organization. Whereas a manager may be responsible for one functional area, the _____ is responsible for all areas.

a. General manager
b. Chief technology officer
c. Chief knowledge officer
d. Managing director

7. In human resources or industrial/organizational psychology, _____' 'multisource feedback,' or 'multisource assessment,' is feedback that comes from all around an employee. '360' refers to the 360 degrees in a circle, with an individual figuratively in the center of the circle. Feedback is provided by subordinates, peers, and supervisors.

a. Personnel management
b. Job knowledge
c. Revolving door syndrome
d. 360-degree feedback

8. _____ consists of the sale of goods or merchandise from a fixed location, such as a department store, boutique or kiosk in small or individual lots for direct consumption by the purchaser. _____ may include subordinated services, such as delivery. Purchasers may be individuals or businesses.

a. Planogram
b. 1990 Clean Air Act
c. 28-hour day
d. Retailing

9. _____ is a concept related to the relative abilities of parties in a situation to exert influence over each other. If both parties are on an equal footing in a debate, then they will have equal _____, such as in a perfectly competitive market, or between an evenly matched monopoly and monopsony.

There are a number of fields where the concept of _____ has proven crucial to coherent analysis: game theory, labour economics, collective bargaining arrangements, diplomatic negotiations, settlement of litigation, the price of insurance, and any negotiation in general.

a. Buy-sell agreement
b. 1990 Clean Air Act
c. Bargaining power
d. Trade credit

10. _____ describes the situation when output from (or information about the result of) an event or phenomenon in the past will influence the same event/phenomenon in the present or future. When an event is part of a chain of cause-and-effect that forms a circuit or loop, then the event is said to 'feed back' into itself.

_____ is also a synonym for:

- _____ signal; the information about the initial event that is the basis for subsequent modification of the event.
- _____ loop; the causal path that leads from the initial generation of the _____ signal to the subsequent modification of the event.

_____ is a mechanism, process or signal that is looped back to control a system within itself. Such a loop is called a _____ loop.

a. 1990 Clean Air Act
b. Positive feedback
c. Feedback loop
d. Feedback

Chapter 1. Management and Managers

11. The 'business case for _____', theorizes that in a global marketplace, a company that employs a diverse workforce (both men and women, people of many generations, people from ethnically and racially diverse backgrounds etc.) is better able to understand the demographics of the marketplace it serves and is thus better equipped to thrive in that marketplace than a company that has a more limited range of employee demographics.

An additional corollary suggests that a company that supports the _____ of its workforce can also improve employee satisfaction, productivity and retention.

a. Virtual team
b. Kanban
c. Trademark
d. Diversity

12. _____ in its literal sense is the process of transformation of local or regional phenomena into global ones. It can be described as a process by which the people of the world are unified into a single society and function together.

This process is a combination of economic, technological, sociocultural and political forces.

a. Histogram
b. Cost Management
c. Globalization
d. Collaborative Planning, Forecasting and Replenishment

13. The _____ is the labour pool in employment. It is generally used to describe those working for a single company or industry, but can also apply to a geographic region like a city, country, state, etc. The term generally excludes the employers or management, and implies those involved in manual labour.

a. Workforce
b. Work-life balance
c. Division of labour
d. Pink-collar worker

14. _____ is one of the managerial functions like planning, organizing, staffing and directing. It is an important function because it helps to check the errors and to take the corrective action so that deviation from standards are minimized and stated goals of the organization are achieved in desired manner. According to modern concepts, _____ is a foreseeing action whereas earlier concept of _____ was used only when errors were detected. _____ in management means setting standards, measuring actual performance and taking corrective action.

a. Decision tree pruning
b. Turnover
c. Schedule of reinforcement
d. Control

15. _____ refers to the stock of skills and knowledge embodied in the ability to perform labor so as to produce economic value. It is the skills and knowledge gained by a worker through education and experience. Many early economic theories refer to it simply as labor, one of three factors of production, and consider it to be a fungible resource -- homogeneous and easily interchangeable.
   a. Deflation
   b. Market structure
   c. Productivity management
   d. Human capital

16. The term _____ collectively refers to all resources that determine the value and the competitiveness of an enterprise. As such, it includes as subsets the attributes that concur to building all financial statements as well as the balance sheet.
   a. A Stake in the Outcome
   b. AAAI
   c. A4e
   d. Intellectual capital

17. The _____ of 2002 (Pub.L. 107-204, 116 Stat. 745, enacted July 30, 2002), also known as the Public Company Accounting Reform and Investor Protection Act of 2002 and commonly called Sarbanes-Oxley, Sarbox or SOX, is a United States federal law enacted on July 30, 2002, as a reaction to a number of major corporate and accounting scandals including those affecting Enron, Tyco International, Adelphia, Peregrine Systems and WorldCom.
   a. Sarbanes-Oxley Act of 2002
   b. Fair Labor Standards Act
   c. Letter of credit
   d. Sarbanes-Oxley Act

Chapter 2. Evolution of Management Thought

1. The 'business case for _____', theorizes that in a global marketplace, a company that employs a diverse workforce (both men and women, people of many generations, people from ethnically and racially diverse backgrounds etc.) is better able to understand the demographics of the marketplace it serves and is thus better equipped to thrive in that marketplace than a company that has a more limited range of employee demographics.

An additional corollary suggests that a company that supports the _____ of its workforce can also improve employee satisfaction, productivity and retention.

   a. Virtual team
   b. Trademark
   c. Diversity
   d. Kanban

2. _____ occurs when an individual's thoughts or actions are affected by other people. _____ takes many forms and can be seen in conformity, socialization, peer pressure, obedience, leadership, persuasion, sales, and marketing. Harvard psychologist, Herbert Kelman identified three broad varieties of _____.
   a. Soft skill
   b. Role conflict
   c. Social awareness
   d. Social influence

3. The _____ is the labour pool in employment. It is generally used to describe those working for a single company or industry, but can also apply to a geographic region like a city, country, state, etc. The term generally excludes the employers or management, and implies those involved in manual labour.
   a. Workforce
   b. Division of labour
   c. Work-life balance
   d. Pink-collar worker

4. _____ is one of the managerial functions like planning, organizing, staffing and directing. It is an important function because it helps to check the errors and to take the corrective action so that deviation from standards are minimized and stated goals of the organization are achieved in desired manner. According to modern concepts, _____ is a foreseeing action whereas earlier concept of _____ was used only when errors were detected. _____ in management means setting standards, measuring actual performance and taking corrective action.
   a. Turnover
   b. Schedule of reinforcement
   c. Control
   d. Decision tree pruning

Chapter 2. Evolution of Management Thought

5. _____ is a theory of management that analyzes and synthesizes workflows, with the objective of improving labour productivity. The core ideas of the theory were developed by Frederick Winslow Taylor in the 1880s and 1890s, and were first published in his monographs, Shop Management and The Principles of _____ Taylor believed that decisions based upon tradition and rules of thumb should be replaced by precise procedures developed after careful study of an individual at work.

   a. Capacity planning
   b. Value engineering
   c. Master production schedule
   d. Scientific management

6. The sociologist Max Weber defined _____ as 'resting on devotion to the exceptional sanctity, heroism or exemplary character of an individual person, and of the normative patterns or order revealed or ordained by him.' _____ is one of three forms of authority laid out in Weber's tripartite classification of authority, the other two being traditional authority and rational-legal authority. The concept has acquired wide usage among sociologists.

   In his writings about _____, Weber applies the term charisma to 'a certain quality of an individual personality, by virtue of which he is set apart from ordinary men and treated as endowed with supernatural, superhuman, or at least specifically exceptional powers or qualities.

   a. 28-hour day
   b. 1990 Clean Air Act
   c. Charismatic authority
   d. Rational-legal authority

7. _____ is a form of leadership in which the authority of an organization or a ruling regime is largely tied to legal rationality, legal legitimacy and bureaucracy. The majority of the modern states of the twentieth century are rational-legal authorities, according to those who use this form of classification.

   In sociology, the concept of rational-legal domination comes from Max Weber's tripartite classification of authority; the other two forms being traditional authority and charismatic authority.

   a. Rational-legal authority
   b. Traditional authority
   c. 28-hour day
   d. 1990 Clean Air Act

8. _____ is a form of leadership in which the authority of an organization or a ruling regime is largely tied to tradition or custom. The main reason for the given state of affairs is that it 'has always been that way'.

In sociology, the concept of _____ comes from Max Weber's tripartite classification of authority, the other two forms being charismatic authority and rational-legal authority.

a. 28-hour day
b. Rational-legal authority
c. 1990 Clean Air Act
d. Traditional authority

9. The _____ is a form of reactivity whereby subjects improve an aspect of their behavior being experimentally measured simply in response to the fact that they are being studied, not in response to any particular experimental manipulation.

The term was coined in 1955 by Henry A. Landsberger when analyzing older experiments from 1924-1932 at the Hawthorne Works (outside Chicago.) Hawthorne Works had commissioned a study to see if its workers would become more productive in higher or lower levels of light.

a. 1990 Clean Air Act
b. 33 Strategies of War
c. 28-hour day
d. Hawthorne effect

10. _____ and Theory Y are theories of human motivation created and developed by Douglas McGregor at the MIT Sloan School of Management in the 1960s that have been used in human resource management, organizational behavior, organizational communication and organizational development. They describe two very different attitudes toward workforce motivation. McGregor felt that companies followed either one or the other approach.

In _____, which many managers practice, management assumes employees are inherently lazy and will avoid work if they can. They inherently dislike work. Because of this, workers need to be closely supervised and comprehensive systems of controls developed.

a. Theory X
b. Cash cow
c. Job enrichment
d. Management team

Chapter 2. Evolution of Management Thought

11. Theory X and _____ are theories of human motivation created and developed by Douglas McGregor at the MIT Sloan School of Management in the 1960s that have been used in human resource management, organizational behavior, organizational communication and organizational development. They describe two very different attitudes toward workforce motivation. McGregor felt that companies followed either one or the other approach.

In _____, management assumes employees may be ambitious and self-motivated and exercise self-control. It is believed that employees enjoy their mental and physical work duties.

   a. Design leadership
   b. Theory Y
   c. Business Workflow Analysis
   d. Contingency theory

12. _____ in the USA, Canada, South Africa and Australia, and operational research in Europe, is an interdisciplinary branch of applied mathematics and formal science that uses methods such as mathematical modeling, statistics, and algorithms to arrive at optimal or near optimal solutions to complex problems. It is typically concerned with optimizing the maxima (profit, assembly line performance, crop yield, bandwidth, etc) or minima (loss, risk, etc.) of some objective function.

   a. A Stake in the Outcome
   b. Operations research
   c. AAAI
   d. A4e

13. A _____ is a list of the general tasks and responsibilities of a position. Typically, it also includes to whom the position reports, specifications such as the qualifications needed by the person in the job, salary range for the position, etc. A _____ is usually developed by conducting a job analysis, which includes examining the tasks and sequences of tasks necessary to perform the job.

   a. Recruitment
   b. Recruitment advertising
   c. Recruitment Process Insourcing
   d. Job description

14. _____ describes the situation when output from (or information about the result of) an event or phenomenon in the past will influence the same event/phenomenon in the present or future. When an event is part of a chain of cause-and-effect that forms a circuit or loop, then the event is said to 'feed back' into itself.

_____ is also a synonym for:

- _____ signal; the information about the initial event that is the basis for subsequent modification of the event.
- _____ loop; the causal path that leads from the initial generation of the _____ signal to the subsequent modification of the event.

_____ is a mechanism, process or signal that is looped back to control a system within itself. Such a loop is called a _____ loop.

a. Feedback
b. 1990 Clean Air Act
c. Feedback loop
d. Positive feedback

15. _____ is the term used to describe a situation where different entities cooperate advantageously for a final outcome. Simply defined, it means that the whole is greater than the sum of the individual parts. Although the whole will be greater than each individual part, this is not the concept of _____.
a. Synergy
b. 28-hour day
c. 33 Strategies of War
d. 1990 Clean Air Act

16. Various _____ can be employed dependent on the culture of the business, the nature of the task, the nature of the workforce and the personality and skills of the leaders. This idea was further developed by Robert Tannenbaum and Warren H. Schmidt (1958, 1973) who argued that the style of leadership is dependent upon the prevailing circumstance; therefore leaders should exercise a range of leadership styles and should deploy them as appropriate.

An Autocratic or authoritarian manager makes all the decisions, keeping the information and decision making among the senior management.

a. Management styles
b. 33 Strategies of War
c. 1990 Clean Air Act
d. 28-hour day

17. _____ in its literal sense is the process of transformation of local or regional phenomena into global ones. It can be described as a process by which the people of the world are unified into a single society and function together.

Chapter 2. Evolution of Management Thought 11

This process is a combination of economic, technological, sociocultural and political forces.

a. Collaborative Planning, Forecasting and Replenishment
b. Histogram
c. Cost Management
d. Globalization

18. _____ is an inventory strategy that strives to improve the return on investment of a business by reducing in-process inventory and its associated carrying costs. To meet _____ objectives, the process relies on signals between different points in the process. This means the process is often driven by a series of signals, or Kanban , which tell production when to make the next part. Kanban are usually 'tickets' but can be simple visual signals, such as the presence or absence of a part on a shelf. Implemented correctly, _____ can dramatically improve a manufacturing organization's return on investment, quality, and efficiency.
   a. 1990 Clean Air Act
   b. 33 Strategies of War
   c. Just-in-time
   d. 28-hour day

19. The _____ is given by the United States National Institute of Standards and Technology. Through the actions of the National Productivity Advisory Committee chaired by Jack Grayson, it was established by the Malcolm Baldrige National Quality Improvement Act of 1987 - Public Law 100-107 and named for Malcolm Baldrige, who served as United States Secretary of Commerce during the Reagan administration from 1981 until his 1987 death in a rodeo accident. APQC, , organized the first White House Conference on Productivity, spearheading the creation and design of the _____ in 1987, and jointly administering the award for its first three years.
   a. Time and attendance
   b. Business Network Transformation
   c. Scenario planning
   d. Malcolm Baldrige National Quality Award

20. _____ is the name applied to two competing management theories. One was developed by Abraham H. Maslow in his book Maslow on Management and the other is Dr. William Ouchi's so-called 'Japanese Management' style popularized during the Asian economic boom of the 1980s. In contrast Theory X, which stated that workers inherently dislike and avoid work and must be driven to it, and Theory Y, which stated that work is natural and can be a source of satisfaction when aimed at higher order human psychological needs, _____ focused on increasing employee loyalty to the company by providing a job for life with a strong focus on the well-being of the employee, both on and off the job.

a. 1990 Clean Air Act
b. Theory Z
c. Sustainable competitive advantage
d. 28-hour day

Chapter 3. Social Responsibility and Ethics

1. _____ is a form of corporate self-regulation integrated into a business model. Ideally, _____ policy would function as a built-in, self-regulating mechanism whereby business would monitor and ensure their adherence to law, ethical standards, and international norms. Business would embrace responsibility for the impact of their activities on the environment, consumers, employees, communities, stakeholders and all other members of the public sphere.
   a. 33 Strategies of War
   b. Corporate social responsibility
   c. 1990 Clean Air Act
   d. 28-hour day

2. _____ is subcontracting a process, such as product design or manufacturing, to a third-party company. The decision to outsource is often made in the interest of lowering cost or making better use of time and energy costs, redirecting or conserving energy directed at the competencies of a particular business, or to make more efficient use of land, labor, capital, (information) technology and resources. _____ became part of the business lexicon during the 1980s.
   a. Unemployment insurance
   b. Opinion leadership
   c. Outsourcing
   d. Operant conditioning

3. _____ is a form of applied ethics that examines ethical principles and moral or ethical problems that arise in a business environment. It applies to all aspects of business conduct and is relevant to the conduct of individuals and business organizations as a whole. Applied ethics is a field of ethics that deals with ethical questions in many fields such as medical, technical, legal and _____.
   a. Facilitation payments
   b. Business ethics
   c. Hypernorms
   d. Corporate Sustainability

4. _____ is one of the managerial functions like planning, organizing, staffing and directing. It is an important function because it helps to check the errors and to take the corrective action so that deviation from standards are minimized and stated goals of the organization are achieved in desired manner. According to modern concepts, _____ is a foreseeing action whereas earlier concept of _____ was used only when errors were detected. _____ in management means setting standards, measuring actual performance and taking corrective action.
   a. Turnover
   b. Decision tree pruning
   c. Schedule of reinforcement
   d. Control

5. _____ is the value of objects, both physical objects and abstract objects, not as ends-in-themselves but a means of achieving something else. It is often contrasted with items of intrinsic value.

It is studied in the field of value theory.

a. AAAI
b. Instrumental value
c. A4e
d. A Stake in the Outcome

6. _____ is an idea in the field of Organizational studies and management which describes the psychology, attitudes, experiences, beliefs and Values (personal and cultural values) of an organization. It has been defined as 'the specific collection of values and norms that are shared by people and groups in an organization and that control the way they interact with each other and with stakeholders outside the organization.'

This definition continues to explain organizational values also known as 'beliefs and ideas about what kinds of goals members of an organization should pursue and ideas about the appropriate kinds or standards of behavior organizational members should use to achieve these goals. From organizational values develop organizational norms, guidelines or expectations that prescribe appropriate kinds of behavior by employees in particular situations and control the behavior of organizational members towards one another.'

_____ is not the same as corporate culture.

a. Union shop
b. Organizational development
c. Organizational effectiveness
d. Organizational culture

7. _____ is a term that refers both to:

- a formal discipline used to help appraise, or assess, the case for a project or proposal, which itself is a process known as project appraisal; and
- an informal approach to making decisions of any kind.

Under both definitions the process involves, whether explicitly or implicitly, weighing the total expected costs against the total expected benefits of one or more actions in order to choose the best or most profitable option. The formal process is often referred to as either CBA (_____) or BCost-benefit analysis

A hallmark of CBA is that all benefits and all costs are expressed in money terms, and are adjusted for the time value of money, so that all flows of benefits and flows of project costs over time (which tend to occur at different points in time) are expressed on a common basis in terms of their 'present value.' Closely related, but slightly different, formal techniques include Cost-effectiveness analysis, Economic impact analysis, Fiscal impact analysis and Social Return on Investment(SROI) analysis. The latter builds upon the logic of _____, but differs in that it is explicitly designed to inform the practical decision-making of enterprise managers and investors focused on optimising their social and environmental impacts.

   a. Cost-benefit analysis
   b. Kepner-Tregoe
   c. Gittins index
   d. Decision engineering

8. An _____ is a situation that will often involve an apparent conflict between moral imperatives, in which to obey one would result in transgressing another. This is also called an ethical paradox since in moral philosophy, paradox plays a central role in ethics debates. For instance, an ethical admonition to 'love thy neighbour as thy self' is not always just in contrast with, but sometimes in contradiction to an armed neighbour actively trying to kill you: if he or she succeeds, you will not be able to love him or her.
   a. A Stake in the Outcome
   b. Ethical dilemma
   c. AAAI
   d. A4e

9. In economics, _____ is a measure of the relative satisfaction from consumption of various goods and services. Given this measure, one may speak meaningfully of increasing or decreasing _____, and thereby explain economic behavior in terms of attempts to increase one's _____. For illustrative purposes, changes in _____ are sometimes expressed in units called utils.
   a. Indirect utility function
   b. A Stake in the Outcome
   c. Ordinal utility
   d. Utility

10. _____ is the strategic and coherent approach to the management of an organisation's most valued assets - the people working there who individually and collectively contribute to the achievement of the objectives of the business. The terms '_____' and 'human resources' (HR) have largely replaced the term 'personnel management' as a description of the processes involved in managing people in organizations. In simple sense, _____ means employing people, developing their resources, utilizing, maintaining and compensating their services in tune with the job and organizational requirement.

a. Revolving door syndrome
b. Job knowledge
c. Progressive discipline
d. Human resource management

11. The _____ is an American federal law which allows people who are not affiliated with the government to file actions against federal contractors claiming fraud against the government. The act of filing such actions is informally called 'whistleblowing.' Persons filing under the Act stand to receive a portion (usually about 15-25 percent) of any recovered damages.
   a. Personal Responsibility and Work Opportunity Reconciliation Act
   b. Bennett Amendment
   c. Chrapliwy v. Uniroyal
   d. False Claims Act

12. The _____ of 2002 (Pub.L. 107-204, 116 Stat. 745, enacted July 30, 2002), also known as the Public Company Accounting Reform and Investor Protection Act of 2002 and commonly called Sarbanes-Oxley, Sarbox or SOX, is a United States federal law enacted on July 30, 2002, as a reaction to a number of major corporate and accounting scandals including those affecting Enron, Tyco International, Adelphia, Peregrine Systems and WorldCom.
   a. Sarbanes-Oxley Act of 2002
   b. Fair Labor Standards Act
   c. Letter of credit
   d. Sarbanes-Oxley Act

Chapter 4. Strategic Management and Planning in a Global Environment

1. _____ is an organization's process of defining its strategy and making decisions on allocating its resources to pursue this strategy, including its capital and people. Various business analysis techniques can be used in _____, including SWOT analysis (Strengths, Weaknesses, Opportunities, and Threats) and PEST analysis (Political, Economic, Social, and Technological analysis) or STEER analysis involving Socio-cultural, Technological, Economic, Ecological, and Regulatory factors and EPISTEL (Environment, Political, Informatic, Social, Technological, Economic and Legal)

_____ is the formal consideration of an organization's future course. All _____ deals with at least one of three key questions:

1. 'What do we do?'
2. 'For whom do we do it?'
3. 'How do we excel?'

In business _____, the third question is better phrased 'How can we beat or avoid competition?'. (Bradford and Duncan, page 1.)

a. 33 Strategies of War
b. Strategic planning
c. 1990 Clean Air Act
d. 28-hour day

2. _____ is one of the managerial functions like planning, organizing, staffing and directing. It is an important function because it helps to check the errors and to take the corrective action so that deviation from standards are minimized and stated goals of the organization are achieved in desired manner. According to modern concepts, _____ is a foreseeing action whereas earlier concept of _____ was used only when errors were detected. _____ in management means setting standards, measuring actual performance and taking corrective action.

a. Control
b. Turnover
c. Schedule of reinforcement
d. Decision tree pruning

3. A _____ is a brief written statement of the purpose of a company or organization. Ideally, a _____ guides the actions of the organization, spells out its overall goal, provides a sense of direction, and guides decision making for all levels of management.

_____s often contain the following:

- Purpose and aim of the organization
- The organization's primary stakeholders: clients, stockholders, etc.
- Responsibilities of the organization toward these stakeholders
- Products and services offered

Chapter 4. Strategic Management and Planning in a Global Environment

In developing a _____:

- Encourage as much input as feasible from employees, volunteers, and other stakeholders
- Publicize it broadly

The _____ can be used to resolve differences between business stakeholders. Stakeholders include: employees including managers and executives, stockholders, board of directors, customers, suppliers, distributors, creditors, governments (local, state, federal, etc.), unions, competitors, NGO's, and the general public.

a. 33 Strategies of War
b. 1990 Clean Air Act
c. 28-hour day
d. Mission statement

4. _____ in its literal sense is the process of transformation of local or regional phenomena into global ones. It can be described as a process by which the people of the world are unified into a single society and function together.

This process is a combination of economic, technological, sociocultural and political forces.

a. Histogram
b. Collaborative Planning, Forecasting and Replenishment
c. Cost Management
d. Globalization

5. A _____ is the subset of the market on which a specific product is focusing on; Therefore the market niche defines the specific product features aimed at satisfying specific market needs, as well as the price range, production quality and the demographics that is intended to impact.

Every single product that is on sale can be defined by its _____. As of special note, the products aimed at a wide demographics audience, with the resulting low price (due to Price elasticity of demand), are said to belong to the Mainstream niche, in practice referred only as Mainstream or of high demand.

a. Private placement
b. Choquet integral
c. Niche market
d. Labor intensive

Chapter 4. Strategic Management and Planning in a Global Environment

6. _____ describes commerce transactions between businesses, such as between a manufacturer and a wholesaler, or between a wholesaler and a retailer. Contrasting terms are business-to-consumer (B2C) and business-to-government (B2G.)

The volume of B2B transactions is much higher than the volume of B2C transactions.

a. Category management
b. Product bundling
c. Market environment
d. Business-to-business

7. Business-to-consumer describes activities of businesses serving end consumers with products and/or services.

An example of a _____ transaction would be a person buying a pair of shoes from a retailer. The transactions that led to the shoes being available for purchase, that is the purchase of the leather, laces, rubber, etc.

a. B2C
b. PEST analysis
c. Market environment
d. Green marketing

8. The 'business case for _____', theorizes that in a global marketplace, a company that employs a diverse workforce (both men and women, people of many generations, people from ethnically and racially diverse backgrounds etc.) is better able to understand the demographics of the marketplace it serves and is thus better equipped to thrive in that marketplace than a company that has a more limited range of employee demographics.

An additional corollary suggests that a company that supports the _____ of its workforce can also improve employee satisfaction, productivity and retention.

a. Virtual team
b. Kanban
c. Trademark
d. Diversity

9. The _____ of 2002 (Pub.L. 107-204, 116 Stat. 745, enacted July 30, 2002), also known as the Public Company Accounting Reform and Investor Protection Act of 2002 and commonly called Sarbanes-Oxley, Sarbox or SOX, is a United States federal law enacted on July 30, 2002, as a reaction to a number of major corporate and accounting scandals including those affecting Enron, Tyco International, Adelphia, Peregrine Systems and WorldCom.

a. Letter of credit
b. Sarbanes-Oxley Act
c. Sarbanes-Oxley Act of 2002
d. Fair Labor Standards Act

10. _____ is a concept related to the relative abilities of parties in a situation to exert influence over each other. If both parties are on an equal footing in a debate, then they will have equal _____, such as in a perfectly competitive market, or between an evenly matched monopoly and monopsony.

There are a number of fields where the concept of _____ has proven crucial to coherent analysis: game theory, labour economics, collective bargaining arrangements, diplomatic negotiations, settlement of litigation, the price of insurance, and any negotiation in general.

a. Buy-sell agreement
b. Trade credit
c. 1990 Clean Air Act
d. Bargaining power

11. In mainstream economic theories, the supply of labor is the number of total hours that workers wish to work at a given real wage rate. Realisticly, the _____ is a fuction of various factors within an economy. For instance, overpopulation increases the number of available workers driving down wages and can result in high unemployment.
a. 28-hour day
b. 33 Strategies of War
c. 1990 Clean Air Act
d. Labor supply

12. _____ is, in very basic words, a position a firm occupies against its competitors.

According to Michael Porter, the three methods for creating a sustainable _____ are through:

1. Cost leadership

2. Differentiation

3. Focus (economics)

a. 28-hour day
b. Theory Z
c. 1990 Clean Air Act
d. Competitive advantage

13. In economics, business, retail, and accounting, a _____ is the value of money that has been used up to produce something, and hence is not available for use anymore. In economics, a _____ is an alternative that is given up as a result of a decision. In business, the _____ may be one of acquisition, in which case the amount of money expended to acquire it is counted as _____.
   a. Fixed costs
   b. Cost allocation
   c. Cost overrun
   d. Cost

14. _____ is a concept developed by Michael Porter, used in business strategy. It describes a way to establish the competitive advantage. _____, in basic words, means the lowest cost of operation in the industry.
   a. Strategic business unit
   b. Cost leadership
   c. Switching cost
   d. Strategic group

15. _____ has been described as the 'process of social influence in which one person can enlist the aid and support of others in the accomplishment of a common task'. A definition more inclusive of followers comes from Alan Keith of Genentech who said '_____ is ultimately about creating a way for people to contribute to making something extraordinary happen.'

_____ is one of the most salient aspects of the organizational context. However, defining _____ has been challenging.

   a. 28-hour day
   b. 1990 Clean Air Act
   c. Leadership
   d. Situational leadership

Chapter 4. Strategic Management and Planning in a Global Environment

16. _____ of the learning curve effect and the closely related experience curve effect express the relationship between equations for experience and efficiency or between efficiency gains and investment in the effort. The experience of 'learning curves' was first observed by the 19th Century German psychologist Hermann Ebbinghaus according to the difficulty of memorizing varying numbers of verbal stimuli, and subsequent learning about the complex processes of learning are discussed in the

The rule used for representing the learning curve effect states that the more times a task has been performed, the less time will be required on each subsequent iteration.

a. Point biserial correlation coefficient
b. Spatial Decision Support Systems
c. Distribution
d. Models

17. A _____ is an arrangement of qualitative or quantitative values in rows and columns that allows an analyst to systematically identify, analyze, and rate the strength of relationships between sets of information. Elements of a _____ represent decisions based on certain decision criteria. The matrix is especially useful for looking at large numbers of decision factors and assessing each factor's relative importance.

a. Decision matrix
b. Multi-Criteria Decision Analysis
c. Decision-matrix method
d. Health management system

18. _____ describes the situation when output from (or information about the result of) an event or phenomenon in the past will influence the same event/phenomenon in the present or future. When an event is part of a chain of cause-and-effect that forms a circuit or loop, then the event is said to 'feed back' into itself.

_____ is also a synonym for:

- _____ signal; the information about the initial event that is the basis for subsequent modification of the event.
- _____ loop; the causal path that leads from the initial generation of the _____ signal to the subsequent modification of the event.

_____ is a mechanism, process or signal that is looped back to control a system within itself. Such a loop is called a _____ loop.

Chapter 4. Strategic Management and Planning in a Global Environment 23

a. Positive feedback
b. 1990 Clean Air Act
c. Feedback loop
d. Feedback

19. A broad definition of _____ is the action of gathering, analyzing, and distributing information about products, customers, competitors and any aspect of the environment needed to support executives and managers in making strategic decisions for an organization.

Key points of this definitions:

1. _____ is an ethical and legal business practice. (This is important as _____ professionals emphasize that the discipline is not the same as industrial espionage which is both unethical and usually illegal.)
2. The focus is on the external business environment.
3. There is a process involved in gathering information, converting it into intelligence and then utilizing this in business decision making. _____ professionals emphasize that if the intelligence gathered is not usable (or actionable) then it is not intelligence.

A more focused definition of _____ regards it as the organizational function responsible for the early identification of risks and opportunities in the market before they become obvious. Experts also call this process the early signal analysis. This definition focuses attention on the difference between dissemination of widely available factual information (such as market statistics, financial reports, newspaper clippings) performed by functions such as libraries and information centers, and _____ which is a perspective on developments and events aimed at yielding a competitive edge.

a. Competitive intelligence
b. Competitor or Competitive Intelligence
c. 1990 Clean Air Act
d. 28-hour day

Chapter 5. Planning in the Contemporary Organization

1. A _____ is a name or trademark connected with a product or producer. _____s have become increasingly important components of culture and the economy, now being described as 'cultural accessories and personal philosophies'.

   Some people distinguish the psychological aspect of a _____ from the experiential aspect.
   a. Brand loyalty
   b. Brand awareness
   c. Brand extension
   d. Brand

2. _____ is one of the managerial functions like planning, organizing, staffing and directing. It is an important function because it helps to check the errors and to take the corrective action so that deviation from standards are minimized and stated goals of the organization are achieved in desired manner. According to modern concepts, _____ is a foreseeing action whereas earlier concept of _____ was used only when errors were detected. _____ in management means setting standards, measuring actual performance and taking corrective action.
   a. Schedule of reinforcement
   b. Decision tree pruning
   c. Turnover
   d. Control

3. _____ can be regarded as an outcome of mental processes (cognitive process) leading to the selection of a course of action among several alternatives. Every _____ process produces a final choice. The output can be an action or an opinion of choice.
   a. 1990 Clean Air Act
   b. 28-hour day
   c. 33 Strategies of War
   d. Decision making

4. In economics, business, retail, and accounting, a _____ is the value of money that has been used up to produce something, and hence is not available for use anymore. In economics, a _____ is an alternative that is given up as a result of a decision. In business, the _____ may be one of acquisition, in which case the amount of money expended to acquire it is counted as _____.
   a. Cost overrun
   b. Fixed costs
   c. Cost allocation
   d. Cost

Chapter 5. Planning in the Contemporary Organization

5. _____ is an organization's process of defining its strategy and making decisions on allocating its resources to pursue this strategy, including its capital and people. Various business analysis techniques can be used in _____, including SWOT analysis (Strengths, Weaknesses, Opportunities, and Threats) and PEST analysis (Political, Economic, Social, and Technological analysis) or STEER analysis involving Socio-cultural, Technological, Economic, Ecological, and Regulatory factors and EPISTEL (Environment, Political, Informatic, Social, Technological, Economic and Legal)

_____ is the formal consideration of an organization's future course. All _____ deals with at least one of three key questions:

1. 'What do we do?'
2. 'For whom do we do it?'
3. 'How do we excel?'

In business _____, the third question is better phrased 'How can we beat or avoid competition?'. (Bradford and Duncan, page 1.)

a. 33 Strategies of War
b. Strategic planning
c. 28-hour day
d. 1990 Clean Air Act

6. _____ is understood as a business unit within the overall corporate identity which is distinguishable from other business because it serves a defined external market where management can conduct strategic planning in relation to products and markets. When companies become really large, they are best thought of as being composed of a number of businesses (or _____s.)

In the broader domain of strategic management, the phrase '_____' came into use in the 1960s, largely as a result of General Electric's many units.

a. Strategic group
b. Strategic drift
c. Switching cost
d. Strategic business unit

7. An _____ is a subset of strategic work plan. It describes short-term ways of achieving milestones and explains how, or what portion of, a strategic plan will be put into operation during a given operational period, in the case of commercial application, a fiscal year or another given budgetary term. An operational plan is the basis for, and justification of an annual operating budget request.

Chapter 5. Planning in the Contemporary Organization

a. Operational planning
b. A Stake in the Outcome
c. AAAI
d. A4e

8. A _____ is a set of instructions having the force of a directive, covering those features of operations that lend themselves to a definite or standardized procedure without loss of effectiveness. Standard Operating Policies and Procedures can be effective catalysts to drive performance improvement and improving organizational results.
   a. Longitudinal study
   b. 1990 Clean Air Act
   c. Risk-benefit analysis
   d. Standard operating procedure

9. _____ generally refers to a list of all planned expenses and revenues. It is a plan for saving and spending. A _____ is an important concept in microeconomics, which uses a _____ line to illustrate the trade-offs between two or more goods.
   a. 28-hour day
   b. 33 Strategies of War
   c. Budget
   d. 1990 Clean Air Act

10. _____ refers to the movement of cash into or out of a business or financial product. It is usually measured during a specified, finite period of time. Measurement of _____ can be used

   - to determine a project's rate of return or value. The time of _____s into and out of projects are used as inputs in financial models such as internal rate of return, and net present value.
   - to determine problems with a business's liquidity. Being profitable does not necessarily mean being liquid. A company can fail because of a shortage of cash, even while profitable.
   - as an alternate measure of a business's profits when it is believed that accrual accounting concepts do not represent economic realities. For example, a company may be notionally profitable but generating little operational cash (as may be the case for a company that barters its products rather than selling for cash.) In such a case, the company may be deriving additional operating cash by issuing shares evaluating default risk, re-investment requirements, etc.

   _____ is a generic term used differently depending on the context. It may be defined by users for their own purposes.

a. Sweat equity
b. Gross profit
c. Cash flow
d. Gross profit margin

11. _____ is a process of agreeing upon objectives within an organization so that management and employees agree to the objectives and understand what they are in the organization.

The term '_____' was first popularized by Peter Drucker in his 1954 book 'The Practice of Management'.

The essence of _____ is participative goal setting, choosing course of actions and decision making.

a. Job enrichment
b. Clean sheet review
c. Business economics
d. Management by objectives

12. The _____ is a performance management tool for measuring whether the smaller-scale operational activities of a company are aligned with its larger-scale objectives in terms of vision and strategy.

By focusing not only on financial outcomes but also on the operational, marketing and developmental inputs to these, the _____ helps provide a more comprehensive view of a business, which in turn helps organizations act in their best long-term interests. This tool is also being used to address business response to climate change and greenhouse gas emissions.

a. Middle management
b. Commercial management
c. Balanced Scorecard
d. Management development

13. _____ is the process whereby an organization establishes the parameters within which programs, investments, and acquisitions are reaching the desired results. Performance Reference Model of the Federal Enterprise Architecture, 2005.

This process of measuring performance often requires the use of statistical evidence to determine progress toward specific defined organizational objectives.

There are many types of measurements.

Chapter 5. Planning in the Contemporary Organization

a. CIFMS
b. Workflow
c. Crisis management
d. Performance measurement

14. In computing, an _____ is the environment in which users run programs, whether in a command-line interface, such as in MS-DOS or the Unix shell such as in the Macintosh operating system the first version of Microsoft Windows, Windows 1.0, was not a full operating system, but a GUI laid over DOS albeit with an API of its own.

a. AAAI
b. A4e
c. A Stake in the Outcome
d. Operating environment

15. In economics, _____ is the desire to own something and the ability to pay for it. The term _____ signifies the ability or the willingness to buy a particular commodity at a given point of time.

a. 1990 Clean Air Act
b. 28-hour day
c. 33 Strategies of War
d. Demand

16. _____ is a structured approach to transitioning individuals, teams, and organizations from a current state to a desired future state. The current definition of _____ includes both organizational _____ processes and individual _____ models, which together are used to manage the people side of change.

A number of models are available for understanding the transitioning of individuals through the phases of _____ and strengthening organizational development initiative in both government and corporate sectors.

a. 1990 Clean Air Act
b. Change management
c. 28-hour day
d. 33 Strategies of War

17. The 'business case for _____', theorizes that in a global marketplace, a company that employs a diverse workforce (both men and women, people of many generations, people from ethnically and racially diverse backgrounds etc.) is better able to understand the demographics of the marketplace it serves and is thus better equipped to thrive in that marketplace than a company that has a more limited range of employee demographics.

An additional corollary suggests that a company that supports the _____ of its workforce can also improve employee satisfaction, productivity and retention.

a. Virtual team
b. Diversity
c. Kanban
d. Trademark

18. Recent strategic thought points ever more clearly towards the conclusion that the critical strategic question is not 'What?,' but 'Why?' The work of Mintzberg and others who draw a distinction between strategic planning (defined as systematic programming of pre-identified strategies) and _____ supports that conclusion. Intensified exploration of strategy from new directions is now coming together in the concept of what is being called _____. At this point, there is no generally accepted definition of the term, no common agreement as to its role or importance, and no standardized list of key competencies of strategic thinkers.

a. Switching cost
b. Strategic drift
c. Strategic thinking
d. Complementors

Chapter 6. Managerial Decision Making

1. _____ can be regarded as an outcome of mental processes (cognitive process) leading to the selection of a course of action among several alternatives. Every _____ process produces a final choice. The output can be an action or an opinion of choice.
   a. 28-hour day
   b. Decision making
   c. 1990 Clean Air Act
   d. 33 Strategies of War

2. _____ is a group creativity technique designed to generate a large number of ideas for the solution of a problem. The method was first popularized in the late 1930s by Alex Faickney Osborn in a book called Applied Imagination. Osborn proposed that groups could double their creative output with _____.
   a. Affiliation
   b. Abraham Harold Maslow
   c. Adam Smith
   d. Brainstorming

3. The _____ is a systematic, interactive forecasting method which relies on a panel of independent experts. The carefully selected experts answer questionnaires in two or more rounds. After each round, a facilitator provides an anonymous summary of the experts' forecasts from the previous round as well as the reasons they provided for their judgments.
   a. Hoshin Kanri
   b. Delphi method
   c. Quality function deployment
   d. Learning organization

4. The _____ is a decision making method for use among groups of many sizes, who want to make their decision quickly, as by a vote, but want everyone's opinions taken into account (as opposed to traditional voting, where only the largest group is considered) . The method of tallying is the difference. First, every member of the group gives their view of the solution, with a short explanation.
   a. Belief decision matrix
   b. Hierarchical Decision Process
   c. Decision model
   d. Nominal group technique

5. _____ consists of the mental process of thinking involved with the process of judging the merits of multiple options and selecting one of them for action. Some simple examples include deciding whether to get up in the morning or go back to sleep, or selecting a given route for a journey. More complex examples (often decisions that affect what a person thinks or their core beliefs) include choosing a lifestyle, religious affiliation, or political position.

Chapter 6. Managerial Decision Making

a. Trade study
b. Choice
c. Groups decision making
d. Championship mobilization

6. _____ describes the situation when output from (or information about the result of) an event or phenomenon in the past will influence the same event/phenomenon in the present or future. When an event is part of a chain of cause-and-effect that forms a circuit or loop, then the event is said to 'feed back' into itself.

_____ is also a synonym for:

- _____ signal; the information about the initial event that is the basis for subsequent modification of the event.
- _____ loop; the causal path that leads from the initial generation of the _____ signal to the subsequent modification of the event.

_____ is a mechanism, process or signal that is looped back to control a system within itself. Such a loop is called a _____ loop.

a. 1990 Clean Air Act
b. Feedback loop
c. Positive feedback
d. Feedback

7. _____ is one of the managerial functions like planning, organizing, staffing and directing. It is an important function because it helps to check the errors and to take the corrective action so that deviation from standards are minimized and stated goals of the organization are achieved in desired manner. According to modern concepts, _____ is a foreseeing action whereas earlier concept of _____ was used only when errors were detected. _____ in management means setting standards, measuring actual performance and taking corrective action.

a. Schedule of reinforcement
b. Decision tree pruning
c. Turnover
d. Control

8. Appraisal is the third and last stage in using formal decision methods. The objective of the appraisal stage is for the decision maker to develop insight into the decision and determine a clear course of action. Much of the insight developed in this stage results from exploring the implications of the formal _____ developed during the formulation stage (i.e., from mining the model.)

Chapter 6. Managerial Decision Making

a. Nominal group technique
b. Decision Matrix
c. Decision model
d. Kepner-Tregoe

9. _____ of the learning curve effect and the closely related experience curve effect express the relationship between equations for experience and efficiency or between efficiency gains and investment in the effort. The experience of 'learning curves' was first observed by the 19th Century German psychologist Hermann Ebbinghaus according to the difficulty of memorizing varying numbers of verbal stimuli, and subsequent learning about the complex processes of learning are discussed in the

.

The rule used for representing the learning curve effect states that the more times a task has been performed, the less time will be required on each subsequent iteration.

a. Point biserial correlation coefficient
b. Models
c. Distribution
d. Spatial Decision Support Systems

10. _____ is a concept based on the fact that rationality of individuals is limited by the information they have, the cognitive limitations of their minds, and the finite amount of time they have to make decisions. This contrasts with the concept of rationality as optimization. Another way to look at _____ is that, because decision-makers lack the ability and resources to arrive at the optimal solution, they instead apply their rationality only after having greatly simplified the choices available.

a. Complete information
b. Mixed strategy
c. Transferable utility
d. Bounded rationality

11. An _____ is a situation that will often involve an apparent conflict between moral imperatives, in which to obey one would result in transgressing another. This is also called an ethical paradox since in moral philosophy, paradox plays a central role in ethics debates. For instance, an ethical admonition to 'love thy neighbour as thy self' is not always just in contrast with, but sometimes in contradiction to an armed neighbour actively trying to kill you: if he or she succeeds, you will not be able to love him or her.

a. AAAI
b. A4e
c. A Stake in the Outcome
d. Ethical dilemma

12. _____ was first described by Barry M. Staw in his 1976 paper, 'Knee deep in the big muddy: A study of escalating commitment to a chosen course of action'. More recently the term Sunk cost fallacy has been used to describe the phenomenon where people justify increased investment in a decision, based on the cumulative prior investment, despite new evidence suggesting that the decision was probably wrong. Such investment may include money, time, or -- in the case of military strategy -- human lives.
   a. A4e
   b. A Stake in the Outcome
   c. Open Options
   d. Escalation of commitment

13. _____ is decision making in groups consisting of multiple members/entities. The challenge of group decision is deciding what action a group should take. There are various systems designed to solve this problem.
   a. Groups decision making
   b. Genbutsu
   c. Control of Substances Hazardous to Health Regulations 2002
   d. Collaborative Planning, Forecasting and Replenishment

14. _____ is a type of thought exhibited by group members who try to minimize conflict and reach consensus without critically testing, analyzing, and evaluating ideas. Individual creativity, uniqueness, and independent thinking are lost in the pursuit of group cohesiveness, as are the advantages of reasonable balance in choice and thought that might normally be obtained by making decisions as a group. During _____, members of the group avoid promoting viewpoints outside the comfort zone of consensus thinking.
   a. Groupthink
   b. Self-report inventory
   c. Psychological statistics
   d. Diffusion of responsibility

15. _____ is the pursuit of influencing outcomes -- including public-policy and resource allocation decisions within political, economic, and social systems and institutions -- that directly affect people's current lives. (Cohen, 2001)

Therefore, _____ can be seen as a deliberate process of speaking out on issues of concern in order to exert some influence on behalf of ideas or persons. Based on this definition, Cohen (2001) states that 'ideologues of all persuasions advocate' to bring a change in people's lives.

a. AAAI
b. A4e
c. A Stake in the Outcome
d. Advocacy

16. The _____ is a chart that had been created by Bruce Henderson for the Boston Consulting Group in 1970 to help corporations with analyzing their business units or product lines. This helps the company allocate resources and is used as an analytical tool in brand marketing, product management, strategic management, and portfolio analysis. _____

To use the chart, analysts plot a scatter graph to rank the business units (or products) on the basis of their relative market shares and growth rates.

a. BCG matrix
b. Marketing plan
c. Marketing strategy
d. Market segment

17. In business, a _____ is a product or a business unit that generates unusually high profit margins: so high that it is responsible for a large amount of a company's operating profit. This profit far exceeds the amount necessary to maintain the _____ business, and the excess is used by the business for other purposes.

A firm is said to be acting as a _____ when its earnings per share (EPS) is equal to its dividends per share (DPS), or in other words, when a firm pays out 100% of its free cash flow (FCF) to its shareholders as dividends at the end of each accounting term.

a. Workflow
b. Cash cow
c. Design management in organization
d. Middle management

18. The _____ (Situation, Task, Action, Result) format is a job interview technique used by interviewers to gather all the relevant information about a specific capability that the job requires. This interview format is said to have a higher degree of predictability of future on-the-job performance than the traditional interview.

- Situation: The interviewer wants you to present a recent challenge and situation in which you found yourself.
- Task: What did you have to achieve? The interviewer will be looking to see what you were trying to achieve from the situation.
- Action: What did you do? The interviewer will be looking for information on what you did, why you did it and what were the alternatives.
- Results: What was the outcome of your actions? What did you achieve through your actions and did you meet your objectives. What did you learn from this experience and have you used this learning since?

a. Phrase completion
b. Competency-based job descriptions
c. Rasch models
d. Star

Chapter 7. Organizing for Effectiveness and Efficiency

1. A _____ is a list of the general tasks and responsibilities of a position. Typically, it also includes to whom the position reports, specifications such as the qualifications needed by the person in the job, salary range for the position, etc. A _____ is usually developed by conducting a job analysis, which includes examining the tasks and sequences of tasks necessary to perform the job.

   a. Recruitment
   b. Recruitment Process Insourcing
   c. Recruitment advertising
   d. Job description

2. In organizational development (OD), _____ is the application of Socio-Technical Systems principles and techniques to the humanization of work.

   The aims of _____ to improved job satisfaction, to improved through-put, to improved quality and to reduced employee problems, e.g., grievances, absenteeism.

   Under scientific management people would be directed by reason and the problems of industrial unrest would be appropriately (i.e., scientifically) addressed.

   a. Graduate recruitment
   b. Management process
   c. Path-goal theory
   d. Work design

3. _____ describes the situation when output from (or information about the result of) an event or phenomenon in the past will influence the same event/phenomenon in the present or future. When an event is part of a chain of cause-and-effect that forms a circuit or loop, then the event is said to 'feed back' into itself.

   _____ is also a synonym for:

   - _____ signal; the information about the initial event that is the basis for subsequent modification of the event.
   - _____ loop; the causal path that leads from the initial generation of the _____ signal to the subsequent modification of the event.

   _____ is a mechanism, process or signal that is looped back to control a system within itself. Such a loop is called a _____ loop.

Chapter 7. Organizing for Effectiveness and Efficiency

a. 1990 Clean Air Act
b. Positive feedback
c. Feedback loop
d. Feedback

4. _____ means increasing the scope of a job through extending the range of its job duties and responsibilities. This contradicts the principles of specialisation and the division of labour whereby work is divided into small units, each of which is performed repetitively by an individual worker. Some motivational theories suggest that the boredom and alienation caused by the division of labour can actually cause efficiency to fall.

   a. Mock interview
   b. Delayering
   c. Job enlargement
   d. Centralization

5. _____ is an attempt to motivate employees by giving them the opportunity to use the range of their abilities. It is an idea that was developed by the American psychologist Frederick Herzberg in the 1950s. It can be contrasted to job enlargement which simply increases the number of tasks without changing the challenge.

   a. Job enrichment
   b. C-A-K-E
   c. Catfish effect
   d. Cash cow

6. _____ refers to training in different ways to improve overall performance. It takes advantage of the particular effectiveness of each training method, while at the same time attempting to neglect the shortcomings of that method by combining it with other methods that address its weaknesses.

Cross training is employee-employer field means, training employees to do one another's work.

   a. 33 Strategies of War
   b. 1990 Clean Air Act
   c. 28-hour day
   d. Cross-training

7. _____ is an approach to management development where an individual is moved through a schedule of assignments designed to give him or her a breadth of exposure to the entire operation.

_____ is also practiced to allow qualified employees to gain more insights into the processes of a company, and to reduce boredom and increase job satisfaction through job variation.

The term _____ can also mean the scheduled exchange of persons in offices, especially in public offices, prior to the end of incumbency or the legislative period.

a. 28-hour day
b. 33 Strategies of War
c. 1990 Clean Air Act
d. Job rotation

8. In a military context, the _____ is the line of authority and responsibility along which orders are passed within a military unit and between different units. The term is also used in a civilian management context describing comparable hierarchical structures of authority.

a. Chain of command
b. 1990 Clean Air Act
c. 28-hour day
d. French leave

9. An _____, or organogram(me)) is a diagram that shows the structure of an organization and the relationships and relative ranks of its parts and positions/jobs. The term is also used for similar diagrams, for example ones showing the different elements of a field of knowledge or a group of languages. The French Encyclopédie had one of the first _____s of knowledge in general.

a. Organizational chart
b. AAAI
c. A Stake in the Outcome
d. A4e

10. An _____ is a mostly hierarchical concept of subordination of entities that collaborate and contribute to serve one common aim.

Organizations are a variant of clustered entities. The structure of an organization is usually set up in many a styles, dependent on their objectives and ambience.

a. Organizational development
b. Open shop
c. Informal organization
d. Organizational structure

Chapter 7. Organizing for Effectiveness and Efficiency

11. The _____ is a standardized, on-scene, all-hazard incident management concept. It is a management protocol originally designed for emergency management agencies in the United States which was later federalized there. It has since been adopted by agencies in other countries.
    a. AAAI
    b. A4e
    c. A Stake in the Outcome
    d. Incident Command Structure

12. _____ is a term originating in military organization theory, but now used more commonly in business management, particularly human resource management. _____ refers to the number of subordinates a supervisor has.

    In the hierarchical business organization of the past it was not uncommon to see average spans of 1 to 10 or even less. That is, one manager supervised ten employees on average.

    a. Senior management
    b. Mentoring
    c. CIFMS
    d. Span of control

13. _____ is one of the managerial functions like planning, organizing, staffing and directing. It is an important function because it helps to check the errors and to take the corrective action so that deviation from standards are minimized and stated goals of the organization are achieved in desired manner. According to modern concepts, _____ is a foreseeing action whereas earlier concept of _____ was used only when errors were detected. _____ in management means setting standards, measuring actual performance and taking corrective action.
    a. Decision tree pruning
    b. Schedule of reinforcement
    c. Control
    d. Turnover

14. _____ is a concept in ethics with several meanings. It is often used synonymously with such concepts as responsibility, answerability, enforcement, blameworthiness, liability and other terms associated with the expectation of account-giving. As an aspect of governance, it has been central to discussions related to problems in both the public and private (corporation) worlds.
    a. A Stake in the Outcome
    b. A4e
    c. Accountability
    d. Usury

Chapter 8. Organizational Design

1. An _____ is a mostly hierarchical concept of subordination of entities that collaborate and contribute to serve one common aim.

Organizations are a variant of clustered entities. The structure of an organization is usually set up in many a styles, dependent on their objectives and ambience.

   a. Open shop
   b. Organizational development
   c. Informal organization
   d. Organizational structure

2. _____ is understood as a business unit within the overall corporate identity which is distinguishable from other business because it serves a defined external market where management can conduct strategic planning in relation to products and markets. When companies become really large, they are best thought of as being composed of a number of businesses (or _____s.)

In the broader domain of strategic management, the phrase '_____' came into use in the 1960s, largely as a result of General Electric's many units.

   a. Strategic group
   b. Switching cost
   c. Strategic business unit
   d. Strategic drift

3. _____ is a dynamic of being mutually and physically responsible to and sharing a common set of principles with others. This concept differs distinctly from 'dependence' in that an interdependent relationship implies that all participants are emotionally, economically, ecologically and or morally 'interdependent.' Some people advocate freedom or independence as a sort of ultimate good; others do the same with devotion to one's family, community, or society. _____ recognizes the truth in each position and weaves them together.
   a. Interdependence
   b. AAAI
   c. A Stake in the Outcome
   d. A4e

4. A _____ -- also known as a geographically dispersed team -- is a group of individuals who work across time, space, and organizational boundaries with links strengthened by webs of communication technology. They have complementary skills and are committed to a common purpose, have interdependent performance goals, and share an approach to work for which they hold themselves mutually accountable. Geographically dispersed teams allow organizations to hire and retain the best people regardless of location.

a. Kanban
b. Virtual team
c. Risk management
d. Trademark

5. _____ can be regarded as an outcome of mental processes (cognitive process) leading to the selection of a course of action among several alternatives. Every _____ process produces a final choice. The output can be an action or an opinion of choice.
   a. 1990 Clean Air Act
   b. 28-hour day
   c. 33 Strategies of War
   d. Decision making

6. _____ is one of the managerial functions like planning, organizing, staffing and directing. It is an important function because it helps to check the errors and to take the corrective action so that deviation from standards are minimized and stated goals of the organization are achieved in desired manner. According to modern concepts, _____ is a foreseeing action whereas earlier concept of _____ was used only when errors were detected. _____ in management means setting standards, measuring actual performance and taking corrective action.
   a. Schedule of reinforcement
   b. Turnover
   c. Decision tree pruning
   d. Control

7. _____ is an idea in the field of Organizational studies and management which describes the psychology, attitudes, experiences, beliefs and Values (personal and cultural values) of an organization. It has been defined as 'the specific collection of values and norms that are shared by people and groups in an organization and that control the way they interact with each other and with stakeholders outside the organization.'

This definition continues to explain organizational values also known as 'beliefs and ideas about what kinds of goals members of an organization should pursue and ideas about the appropriate kinds or standards of behavior organizational members should use to achieve these goals. From organizational values develop organizational norms, guidelines or expectations that prescribe appropriate kinds of behavior by employees in particular situations and control the behavior of organizational members towards one another.'

_____ is not the same as corporate culture.

a. Union shop
b. Organizational effectiveness
c. Organizational development
d. Organizational culture

Chapter 9. Strategic Human Resource Management

1. _____ is the strategic and coherent approach to the management of an organisation's most valued assets - the people working there who individually and collectively contribute to the achievement of the objectives of the business. The terms '_____' and 'human resources' (HR) have largely replaced the term 'personnel management' as a description of the processes involved in managing people in organizations. In simple sense, _____ means employing people, developing their resources, utilizing, maintaining and compensating their services in tune with the job and organizational requirement.
   a. Revolving door syndrome
   b. Progressive discipline
   c. Human resource management
   d. Job knowledge

2. _____ is the process of estimation in unknown situations. Prediction is a similar, but more general term. Both can refer to estimation of time series, cross-sectional or longitudinal data.
   a. 33 Strategies of War
   b. Forecasting
   c. 28-hour day
   d. 1990 Clean Air Act

3. _____ refers to various methodologies for analyzing the requirements of a job.

   The general purpose of _____ is to document the requirements of a job and the work performed. Job and task analysis is performed as a basis for later improvements, including: definition of a job domain; describing a job; developing performance appraisals, selection systems, promotion criteria, training needs assessment, and compensation plans.

   a. Job analysis
   b. Work design
   c. Management process
   d. Hersey-Blanchard situational theory

4. A _____ is a list of the general tasks and responsibilities of a position. Typically, it also includes to whom the position reports, specifications such as the qualifications needed by the person in the job, salary range for the position, etc. A _____ is usually developed by conducting a job analysis, which includes examining the tasks and sequences of tasks necessary to perform the job.
   a. Recruitment advertising
   b. Job description
   c. Recruitment
   d. Recruitment Process Insourcing

Chapter 9. Strategic Human Resource Management

5. _____ is an increasingly broadening term with which an organization, or other human system describes the combination of traditionally administrative personnel functions with acquisition and application of skills, knowledge and experience, Employee Relations and resource planning at various levels. The field draws upon concepts developed in Industrial/Organizational Psychology and System Theory. _____ has at least two related interpretations depending on context. The original usage derives from political economy and economics, where it was traditionally called labor, one of four factors of production although this perspective is changing as a function of new and ongoing research into more strategic approaches at national levels. This first usage is used more in terms of '_____ development', and can go beyond just organizations to the level of nations . The more traditional usage within corporations and businesses refers to the individuals within a firm or agency, and to the portion of the organization that deals with hiring, firing, training, and other personnel issues, typically referred to as `_____ management'.
   a. Progressive discipline
   b. Bradford Factor
   c. Human resource management
   d. Human resources

6. In economics, _____ is the desire to own something and the ability to pay for it. The term _____ signifies the ability or the willingness to buy a particular commodity at a given point of time.
   a. 33 Strategies of War
   b. Demand
   c. 1990 Clean Air Act
   d. 28-hour day

7. _____ is the activity of estimating the quantity of a product or service that consumers will purchase. _____ involves techniques including both informal methods, such as educated guesses, and quantitative methods, such as the use of historical sales data or current data from test markets. _____ may be used in making pricing decisions, in assessing future capacity requirements, or in making decisions on whether to enter a new market.
   a. Profitability index
   b. Demand forecasting
   c. 28-hour day
   d. 1990 Clean Air Act

8. _____ refers to the process of screening, and selecting qualified people for a job at an organization or firm mid- and large-size organizations and companies often retain professional recruiters or outsource some of the process to _____ agencies. External _____ is the process of attracting and selecting employees from outside the organization.

The _____ industry has four main types of agencies: employment agencies, _____ websites and job search engines, 'headhunters' for executive and professional _____, and in-house _____.

Chapter 9. Strategic Human Resource Management

a. Labour hire
b. Referral recruitment
c. Recruitment Process Outsourcing
d. Recruitment

9. A _____ or background investigation is the process of looking up and compiling criminal records, commercial records and financial records (in certain instances such as employment screening) of an individual.

_____s are often requested by employers on job candidates, especially on candidates seeking a position that requires high security or a position of trust, such as in a school, hospital, financial institution, airport, and government (including law enforcement and military.) These checks are traditionally administered by a government agency for a nominal fee, but can also be administered by private companies.

a. Labour productivity
b. Time and attendance
c. Malcolm Baldrige National Quality Award
d. Background check

10. The term _____ in logic applies to arguments or statements.

An argument is valid if and only if the truth of its premises entails the truth of its conclusion, it would be self-contradictory to affirm the premises and deny the conclusion. The corresponding conditional of a valid argument is a logical truth and the negation of its corresponding conditional is a contradiction.

a. 1990 Clean Air Act
b. Simplification
c. Fuzzy logic
d. Validity

11. _____ is a contract between two parties, one being the employer and the other being the employee. An employee may be defined as: 'A person in the service of another under any contract of hire, express or implied, oral or written, where the employer has the power or right to control and direct the employee in the material details of how the work is to be performed.' Black's Law Dictionary page 471 (5th ed. 1979.)

a. Employment counsellor
b. Employment
c. Exit interview
d. Employment rate

12. A _____ is commonly a technical examination of urine, hair, blood, sweat, or oral fluid samples to determine the presence or absence of specified drugs or their metabolized traces.

_____s in the USA can be divided into two general groups, federally and non-federally regulated testing. Federally regulated testing started when Ronald Reagan enacted executive order 12564, requiring all federal employees refrain from using illegal substances in specified DOT regulated occupations.

 a. Drug test
 b. Self-dealing
 c. Postcautionary principle
 d. Resource Conservation and Recovery Act

13. _____ is a method by which the job performance of an employee is evaluated _____ is a part of career development.

_____s are regular reviews of employee performance within organizations

Generally, the aims of a _____ are to:

- Give feedback on performance to employees.
- Identify employee training needs.
- Document criteria used to allocate organizational rewards.
- Form a basis for personnel decisions: salary increases, promotions, disciplinary actions, etc.
- Provide the opportunity for organizational diagnosis and development.
- Facilitate communication between employee and administraton
- Validate selection techniques and human resource policies to meet federal Equal Employment Opportunity requirements.

A common approach to assessing performance is to use a numerical or scalar rating system whereby managers are asked to score an individual against a number of objectives/attributes. In some companies, employees receive assessments from their manager, peers, subordinates and customers while also performing a self assessment.

 a. Progressive discipline
 b. Performance appraisal
 c. Human resource management
 d. Personnel management

14. The _____ refers to a cognitive bias whereby the perception of a particular trait is influenced by the perception of the former traits in a sequence of interpretations.

Chapter 9. Strategic Human Resource Management

Edward L. Thorndike was the first to support the _____ with empirical research. In a psychology study published in 1920, Thorndike asked commanding officers to rate their soldiers; Thorndike found high cross-correlation between all positive and all negative traits.

a. Cognitive biases
b. Distinction bias
c. Sunk costs
d. Halo effect

15. A _____ is a set of categories designed to elicit information about a quantitative or a qualitative attribute. In the social sciences, common examples are the Likert scale and 1-10 _____s in which a person selects the number which is considered to reflect the perceived quality of a product.

A _____ is an instrument that requires the rater to assign the rated object that have numerals assigned to them.

a. Spearman-Brown prediction formula
b. Thurstone scale
c. Rating scale
d. Polytomous Rasch model

16. In economics and sociology, an _____ is any factor (financial or non-financial) that enables or motivates a particular course of action, or counts as a reason for preferring one choice to the alternatives. It is an expectation that encourages people to behave in a certain way. Since human beings are purposeful creatures, the study of _____ structures is central to the study of all economic activity (both in terms of individual decision-making and in terms of co-operation and competition within a larger institutional structure.)

a. AAAI
b. A4e
c. Incentive
d. A Stake in the Outcome

17. In neuroscience, the _____ is a collection of brain structures which attempts to regulate and control behavior by inducing pleasurable effects.

A psychological reward is a process that reinforces behavior -- something that, when offered, causes a behavior to increase in intensity. Reward is an operational concept for describing the positive value an individual ascribes to an object, behavioral act or an internal physical state.

a. 1990 Clean Air Act
b. Reward system
c. 33 Strategies of War
d. 28-hour day

18. _____ is the body of laws, administrative rulings, and precedents which address the legal rights of, and restrictions on, working people and their organizations. As such, it mediates many aspects of the relationship between trade unions, employers and employees. In Canada, employment laws related to unionized workplaces are differentiated from those relating to particular individuals.
   a. Four-day week
   b. Shift work
   c. Labor law
   d. Trade union

19. In employment law, a (BFOQ) (US) or bona fide occupational requirement (BFOR) (Canada) is a quality or an attribute that employers are allowed to consider when making decisions on the hiring and retention of employees - qualities that, when considered, in other contexts would be considered discriminatory and thus violating civil rights employment law.

In employment discrimination law in the United States, United States Code Title 29, Chapter 14 (age discrimination in employment), section 623 (prohibition of age discrimination) establishes that 'It shall not be unlawful for an employer, employment agency, or labor organization (1) to take any action otherwise prohibited under subsections (a), (b), (c), or (e) of this section where age is a _____ reasonably necessary to the normal operation of the particular business, or where the differentiation is based on reasonable factors other than age, or where such practices involve an employee in a workplace in a foreign country, and compliance with such subsections would cause such employer, or a corporation controlled by such employer, to violate the laws of the country in which such workplace is located.'

One example of _____s are mandatory retirement ages for bus drivers and airline pilots, for safety reasons. Further, in advertising, a manufacturer of men's clothing may lawfully advertise for male models.

   a. Corporate governance
   b. MacPherson v. Buick Motor Co.
   c. Bona fide occupational qualification
   d. Sick leave

20. The term _____ was created by President Lyndon B. Johnson when he signed Executive Order 11246 on September 24, 1965, created to prohibit federal contractors from discriminating against employees on the basis of race, sex, creed, religion, color, or national origin. In more recent times, most employers have also added sexual orientation to the list of non-discrimination.

The Executive Order also required contractors to implement affirmative action plans to increase the participation of minorities and women in the workplace.

a. A Stake in the Outcome
b. A4e
c. AAAI
d. Equal Employment Opportunity

21. The U.S. _____ is a federal agency whose goal is ending employment discrimination. The _____ investigates discrimination complaints based on an individual's race, color, national origin, religion, sex, age, disability and retaliation for reporting and/or opposing a discriminatory practice. The Commission is also tasked with filing suits on behalf of alleged victim(s) of discrimination against employers and as an adjudicatory for claims of discrimination brought against federal agencies.

a. ARCO
b. Airbus SAS
c. Airbus Industrie
d. Equal Employment Opportunity Commission

22. The _____ is a United States labor law allowing an employee to take unpaid leave due to a serious health condition that makes the employee unable to perform his job or to care for a sick family member or to care for a new son or daughter (including by birth, adoption or foster care.) The bill was among the first signed into law by President Bill Clinton in his first term.

a. Harvester Judgment
b. Contributory negligence
c. Family and Medical Leave Act of 1993
d. Sarbanes-Oxley Act of 2002

23.

The terms _____ and positive action refer to policies that take race, ethnicity, or gender into consideration in an attempt to promote equal opportunity. The focus of such policies ranges from employment and education to public contracting and health programs. The impetus towards _____ is twofold: to maximize diversity in all levels of society, along with its presumed benefits, and to redress perceived disadvantages due to overt, institutional, or involuntary discrimination.

a. Adam Smith
b. Affirmative action
c. Abraham Harold Maslow
d. Affiliation

24. The 'business case for _____', theorizes that in a global marketplace, a company that employs a diverse workforce (both men and women, people of many generations, people from ethnically and racially diverse backgrounds etc.) is better able to understand the demographics of the marketplace it serves and is thus better equipped to thrive in that marketplace than a company that has a more limited range of employee demographics.

An additional corollary suggests that a company that supports the _____ of its workforce can also improve employee satisfaction, productivity and retention.

a. Trademark
b. Virtual team
c. Kanban
d. Diversity

25. The _____ is the labour pool in employment. It is generally used to describe those working for a single company or industry, but can also apply to a geographic region like a city, country, state, etc. The term generally excludes the employers or management, and implies those involved in manual labour.
a. Pink-collar worker
b. Workforce
c. Work-life balance
d. Division of labour

26. _____ is one of the managerial functions like planning, organizing, staffing and directing. It is an important function because it helps to check the errors and to take the corrective action so that deviation from standards are minimized and stated goals of the organization are achieved in desired manner. According to modern concepts, _____ is a foreseeing action whereas earlier concept of _____ was used only when errors were detected. _____ in management means setting standards, measuring actual performance and taking corrective action.
a. Turnover
b. Decision tree pruning
c. Schedule of reinforcement
d. Control

Chapter 9. Strategic Human Resource Management

27. _____ indicates a more-or-less equal exchange or substitution of goods or services. English speakers often use the term to mean 'a favour for a favour' and the phrases with almost identical meaning include: 'what for what,' 'give and take,' 'tit for tat', 'this for that', and 'you scratch my back, and I'll scratch yours'.

In legal usage, _____ indicates that an item or a service has been traded in return for something of value, usually when the propriety or equity of the transaction is in question.

   a. 1990 Clean Air Act
   b. Quid pro quo
   c. 33 Strategies of War
   d. 28-hour day

28. _____ is unwelcome harassment of a sexual nature, or based upon the receiving party's sex or gender. In some contexts or circumstances, _____ may be illegal. It includes a range of behavior from seemingly mild transgressions and annoyances to actual sexual abuse or sexual assault.
   a. Hypernorms
   b. 28-hour day
   c. 1990 Clean Air Act
   d. Sexual harassment

29. The field of _____ looks at the relationship between management and workers, particularly groups of workers represented by a union.

_____ is an important factor in analyzing 'varieties of capitalism', such as neocorporatism, social democracy, and neoliberalism

   a. Informal organization
   b. Industrial relations
   c. Organizational effectiveness
   d. Overtime

30. The _____ is a 1935 United States federal law that limits the means with which employers may react to workers in the private sector that organize labor unions, engage in collective bargaining, and take part in strikes and other forms of concerted activity in support of their demands. The Act does not, on the other hand, cover those workers who are covered by the Railway Labor Act, agricultural employees, domestic employees, supervisors, independent contractors and some close relatives of individual employers.

It was in a context of severe economic troubles that the Wagner Act came into effect.

a. 33 Strategies of War
b. 1990 Clean Air Act
c. 28-hour day
d. National Labor Relations Act

Chapter 10. Organizational Culture and Change

1. _____ is one of the managerial functions like planning, organizing, staffing and directing. It is an important function because it helps to check the errors and to take the corrective action so that deviation from standards are minimized and stated goals of the organization are achieved in desired manner. According to modern concepts, _____ is a foreseeing action whereas earlier concept of _____ was used only when errors were detected. _____ in management means setting standards, measuring actual performance and taking corrective action.

    a. Control
    b. Schedule of reinforcement
    c. Turnover
    d. Decision tree pruning

2. _____ is an idea in the field of Organizational studies and management which describes the psychology, attitudes, experiences, beliefs and Values (personal and cultural values) of an organization. It has been defined as 'the specific collection of values and norms that are shared by people and groups in an organization and that control the way they interact with each other and with stakeholders outside the organization.'

    This definition continues to explain organizational values also known as 'beliefs and ideas about what kinds of goals members of an organization should pursue and ideas about the appropriate kinds or standards of behavior organizational members should use to achieve these goals. From organizational values develop organizational norms, guidelines or expectations that prescribe appropriate kinds of behavior by employees in particular situations and control the behavior of organizational members towards one another.'

    _____ is not the same as corporate culture.

    a. Union shop
    b. Organizational effectiveness
    c. Organizational development
    d. Organizational culture

3. _____ is an educational process whereby the participant studies their own actions and experience in order to improve performance. This concept is close to learning-by-doing and teaching through examples and repetitions.

    _____ is done in conjunction with others, in small groups called _____ sets or two-in, two-out team.

    a. A4e
    b. Action learning
    c. A Stake in the Outcome
    d. AAAI

Chapter 11. Communicating Effectively within Diverse Organizations

1. _____ describes the situation when output from (or information about the result of) an event or phenomenon in the past will influence the same event/phenomenon in the present or future. When an event is part of a chain of cause-and-effect that forms a circuit or loop, then the event is said to 'feed back' into itself.

   _____ is also a synonym for:

   - _____ signal; the information about the initial event that is the basis for subsequent modification of the event.
   - _____ loop; the causal path that leads from the initial generation of the _____ signal to the subsequent modification of the event.

   _____ is a mechanism, process or signal that is looped back to control a system within itself. Such a loop is called a _____ loop.

   a. Feedback
   b. 1990 Clean Air Act
   c. Positive feedback
   d. Feedback loop

2. _____, e-commuting, e-work, telework, working from home (WFH), or working at home (WAH) is a work arrangement in which employees enjoy flexibility in working location and hours. In other words, the daily commute to a central place of work is replaced by telecommunication links. Many work from home, while others, occasionally also referred to as nomad workers or web commuters utilize mobile telecommunications technology to work from coffee shops or myriad other locations.
   a. 28-hour day
   b. 1990 Clean Air Act
   c. 33 Strategies of War
   d. Telecommuting

3. The 'business case for _____', theorizes that in a global marketplace, a company that employs a diverse workforce (both men and women, people of many generations, people from ethnically and racially diverse backgrounds etc.) is better able to understand the demographics of the marketplace it serves and is thus better equipped to thrive in that marketplace than a company that has a more limited range of employee demographics.

   An additional corollary suggests that a company that supports the _____ of its workforce can also improve employee satisfaction, productivity and retention.

   a. Trademark
   b. Kanban
   c. Diversity
   d. Virtual team

Chapter 12. Leading in a Dynamic Environment

1. _____ has been described as the 'process of social influence in which one person can enlist the aid and support of others in the accomplishment of a common task' . A definition more inclusive of followers comes from Alan Keith of Genentech who said '_____ is ultimately about creating a way for people to contribute to making something extraordinary happen.'

   _____ is one of the most salient aspects of the organizational context. However, defining _____ has been challenging.

   a. 28-hour day
   b. Leadership
   c. 1990 Clean Air Act
   d. Situational leadership

2. _____ is individual power based on a high level of identification with, admiration of, or respect for the powerholder.

   Nationalism, Patriotism, Celebrities and well-respected people are examples of _____ in effect.

   _____ is one of the Five Bases of Social Power, as defined by Bertram Raven and his colleagues[1] in 1959.

   a. Referent power
   b. 28-hour day
   c. 1990 Clean Air Act
   d. 33 Strategies of War

3. Contingency leadership theory in organizational studies is a type of leadership theory, leadership style, and leadership model that presumes that different leadership styles are contingent to different situations. It is also referred as _____ ® theory although, as originally convened, the situational theory term is much more restrictive. The original situational theory argues that the best type of leadership is totally determined by the situational variables.Currently there are many styles of leadership.
   a. 1990 Clean Air Act
   b. Situational theory
   c. 28-hour day
   d. Situational leadership

4. _____ of the learning curve effect and the closely related experience curve effect express the relationship between equations for experience and efficiency or between efficiency gains and investment in the effort. The experience of 'learning curves' was first observed by the 19th Century German psychologist Hermann Ebbinghaus according to the difficulty of memorizing varying numbers of verbal stimuli, and subsequent learning about the complex processes of learning are discussed in the

Chapter 12. Leading in a Dynamic Environment

The rule used for representing the learning curve effect states that the more times a task has been performed, the less time will be required on each subsequent iteration.

a. Spatial Decision Support Systems
b. Models
c. Point biserial correlation coefficient
d. Distribution

5. _____ refers to increasing the spiritual, political, social or economic strength of individuals and communities. It often involves the empowered developing confidence in their own capacities.

The term Human _____ covers a vast landscape of meanings, interpretations, definitions and disciplines ranging from psychology and philosophy to the highly commercialized Self-Help industry and Motivational sciences.

a. A Stake in the Outcome
b. A4e
c. AAAI
d. Empowerment

6. Various _____ can be employed dependent on the culture of the business, the nature of the task, the nature of the workforce and the personality and skills of the leaders. This idea was further developed by Robert Tannenbaum and Warren H. Schmidt (1958, 1973) who argued that the style of leadership is dependent upon the prevailing circumstance; therefore leaders should exercise a range of leadership styles and should deploy them as appropriate.

An Autocratic or authoritarian manager makes all the decisions, keeping the information and decision making among the senior management.

a. 33 Strategies of War
b. Management styles
c. 1990 Clean Air Act
d. 28-hour day

7. _____ is a leadership style that defines as leadership that creates voluble and positive change in the followers. A transformational leader focuses on 'transforming' others to help each other, to look out for each other, be encouraging, harmonious, and look out for the organization as a whole. In this leadership, the leader enhances the motivation, moral and performance of his follower group.

Chapter 12. Leading in a Dynamic Environment

a. SESAMO
b. Strong-Campbell Interest Inventory
c. Polynomial conjoint measurement
d. Transformational leadership

8. _____ , often measured as an _____ Quotient (EQ), is a term that describes the ability, capacity, skill or (in the case of the trait _____ model) a self-perceived ability, to identify, assess, and manage the emotions of one's self, of others, and of groups. Different models have been proposed for the definition of _____ and disagreement exists as to how the term should be used. Despite these disagreements, which are often highly technical, the ability _____ and trait _____ models (but not the mixed models) are enjoying considerable support in the literature and have successful applications in many different domains.
   a. A Stake in the Outcome
   b. A4e
   c. AAAI
   d. Emotional intelligence

Chapter 13. Exploring Individual Differences and Team Dynamics

1. _____ is an advertisement in which a particular product specifically mentions a competitor by name for the express purpose of showing why the competitor is inferior to the product naming it.

This should not be confused with parody advertisements, where a fictional product is being advertised for the purpose of poking fun at the particular advertisement, nor should it be confused with the use of a coined brand name for the purpose of comparing the product without actually naming an actual competitor. ('Wikipedia tastes better and is less filling than the Encyclopedia Galactica.')

In the 1980s, during what has been referred to as the cola wars, soft-drink manufacturer Pepsi ran a series of advertisements where people, caught on hidden camera, in a blind taste test, chose Pepsi over rival Coca-Cola.

a. 1990 Clean Air Act
b. 28-hour day
c. 33 Strategies of War
d. Comparative advertising

2. _____ is a term in psychology which refers to a person's belief about what causes the good or bad results in his or her life, either in general or in a specific area such as health or academics. Understanding of the concept was developed by Julian B. Rotter in 1954, and has since become an important aspect of personality studies.

_____ refers to the extent to which individuals believe that they can control events that affect them.

a. Locus of control
b. Self-enhancement
c. Social loafing
d. Machiavellianism

3. In psychology, _____ reflects a person's overall evaluation or appraisal of his or her own worth.

_____ encompasses beliefs (for example, 'I am competent/incompetent') and emotions (for example, triumph/despair, pride/shame.) Behavior may reflect _____

a. 1990 Clean Air Act
b. 33 Strategies of War
c. Self-esteem
d. 28-hour day

Chapter 13. Exploring Individual Differences and Team Dynamics

4. _____ is one of the managerial functions like planning, organizing, staffing and directing. It is an important function because it helps to check the errors and to take the corrective action so that deviation from standards are minimized and stated goals of the organization are achieved in desired manner. According to modern concepts, _____ is a foreseeing action whereas earlier concept of _____ was used only when errors were detected. _____ in management means setting standards, measuring actual performance and taking corrective action.

   a. Turnover
   b. Schedule of reinforcement
   c. Control
   d. Decision tree pruning

5. The _____ assessment is a psychometric questionnaire designed to measure psychological preferences in how people perceive the world and make decisions.:[1] These preferences were extrapolated from the typological theories originated by Carl Gustav Jung, as published in his 1921 book Psychological Types . The original developers of the personality inventory were Katharine Cook Briggs and her daughter, Isabel Briggs Myers. They began creating the indicator during World War II, believing that a knowledge of personality preferences would help women who were entering the industrial workforce for the first time identify the sort of war-time jobs where they would be 'most comfortable and effective'.:[xiii] The initial questionnaire grew into the _____, which was first published in 1962.

   a. 1990 Clean Air Act
   b. 33 Strategies of War
   c. 28-hour day
   d. Myers-Briggs Type Indicator

6. The _____ is a personality type theory that describes a pattern of behaviors that were once considered to be a risk factor for coronary heart disease. Since its inception in the 1950s, the theory has been widely popularized and also widely criticised for its scientific shortcomings.

   Type A individuals can be described as impatient, excessively time-conscious, insecure about their status, highly competitive, over-ambitious, business-like, hostile, aggressive, incapable of relaxation in taking the smallest issues too seriously; and are somewhat disliked for the way that they're always rushing and demanding other people to serve to their standards of satisfaction.

   a. 33 Strategies of War
   b. 28-hour day
   c. 1990 Clean Air Act
   d. Type A and Type B personality theory

7. In psychology, _____ is a major approach to the study of human personality. Trait theorists are primarily interested in the measurement of traits, which can be defined as habitual patterns of behavior, thought, and emotion. According to this perspective, traits are relatively stable over time, differ among individuals (e.g. some people are outgoing whereas others are shy), and influence behavior.

Chapter 13. Exploring Individual Differences and Team Dynamics

a. Psychometrics
b. Cognitive dissonance
c. Psychological statistics
d. Trait theory

8. _____ is an uncomfortable feeling caused by holding two contradictory ideas simultaneously. The 'ideas' or 'cognitions' in question may include attitudes and beliefs, and also the awareness of one's behavior. The theory of _____ proposes that people have a motivational drive to reduce dissonance by changing their attitudes, beliefs, and behaviors, or by justifying or rationalizing their attitudes, beliefs, and behaviors.

a. Trait theory
b. Quantitative psychology
c. Cognitive dissonance
d. Cognitive bias

9. _____ describes how content an individual is with his or her job.

The happier people are within their job, the more satisfied they are said to be. _____ is not the same as motivation, although it is clearly linked.

a. Goal-setting theory
b. Job satisfaction
c. Human relations
d. Job analysis

10. In mathematics, a _____ law is (roughly speaking) a formal power series behaving as if it were the product of a Lie group. They were first defined in 1946 by S. Bochner. The term _____ sometimes means the same as _____ law, and sometimes means one of several generalizations.

a. 1990 Clean Air Act
b. 28-hour day
c. 33 Strategies of War
d. Formal group

11. _____ is decision making in groups consisting of multiple members/entities. The challenge of group decision is deciding what action a group should take. There are various systems designed to solve this problem.

Chapter 13. Exploring Individual Differences and Team Dynamics

a. Genbutsu
b. Control of Substances Hazardous to Health Regulations 2002
c. Groups decision making
d. Collaborative Planning, Forecasting and Replenishment

12. _____ can be regarded as an outcome of mental processes (cognitive process) leading to the selection of a course of action among several alternatives. Every _____ process produces a final choice. The output can be an action or an opinion of choice.

   a. 1990 Clean Air Act
   b. 28-hour day
   c. Decision making
   d. 33 Strategies of War

13. The 'business case for _____', theorizes that in a global marketplace, a company that employs a diverse workforce (both men and women, people of many generations, people from ethnically and racially diverse backgrounds etc.) is better able to understand the demographics of the marketplace it serves and is thus better equipped to thrive in that marketplace than a company that has a more limited range of employee demographics.

An additional corollary suggests that a company that supports the _____ of its workforce can also improve employee satisfaction, productivity and retention.

   a. Diversity
   b. Trademark
   c. Virtual team
   d. Kanban

14. _____ is a term used in the stock-trading world to describe the practice of buying shares or other securities without actually having the capital to cover the trade. This is possible when recently bought or sold shares are unsettled, and therefore have not been paid for.

Since stock transactions usually settle after three business days, a crafty trader can buy a stock and sell it the following day, without ever having sufficient funds in the account.

   a. Shareholder
   b. Stockholder
   c. Free riding
   d. 1990 Clean Air Act

15. _____ is a type of thought exhibited by group members who try to minimize conflict and reach consensus without critically testing, analyzing, and evaluating ideas. Individual creativity, uniqueness, and independent thinking are lost in the pursuit of group cohesiveness, as are the advantages of reasonable balance in choice and thought that might normally be obtained by making decisions as a group. During _____, members of the group avoid promoting viewpoints outside the comfort zone of consensus thinking.
  a. Diffusion of responsibility
  b. Psychological statistics
  c. Self-report inventory
  d. Groupthink

Chapter 14. Motivating Organizational Members

1. In operant conditioning, _____ occurs when an event following a response causes an increase in the probability of that response occurring in the future. Response strength can be assessed by measures such as the frequency with which the response is made (for example, a pigeon may peck a key more times in the session), or the speed with which it is made (for example, a rat may run a maze faster.) The environment change contingent upon the response is called a reinforcer.

    a. Reinforcement
    b. Diminishing Manufacturing Sources and Material Shortages
    c. Meetings, Incentives, Conferences, and Exhibitions
    d. Historiometry

2. In law, _____ is the term to describe a partnership between two or more parties.

    In England a number of statutes on the subject have been passed, the chief being the Bastardy Act of 1845, and the Bastardy Laws Amendment Acts of 1872 and 1873. The mother of a bastard may summon the putative father to petty sessions within twelve months of the birth (or at any later time if he is proved to have contributed to the child's support within twelve months after the birth), and the justices, as after hearing evidence on both sides, may, if the mother's evidence be corroborated in some material particular, adjudge the man to be the putative father of the child, and order him to pay a sum not exceeding five shillings a week for its maintenance, together with a sum for expenses incidental to the birth, or the funeral expenses, if it has died before the date of order, and the costs of the proceedings.

    a. Affirmative action
    b. Abraham Harold Maslow
    c. Affiliation
    d. Adam Smith

3. Maslow's _____ is a theory in psychology, proposed by Abraham Maslow in his 1943 paper A Theory of Human Motivation, which he subsequently extended to include his observations of humans' innate curiosity.

    Maslow's _____ is predetermined in order of importance. It is often depicted as a pyramid consisting of five levels: the lowest level is associated with physiological needs, while the uppermost level is associated with self-actualization needs, particularly those related to identity and purpose. Deficiency needs must be met first. Once these are met, seeking to satisfy growth needs drives personal growth. The higher needs in this hierarchy only come into focus when the lower needs in the pyramid are met.

    a. Hierarchy of needs
    b. 1990 Clean Air Act
    c. 33 Strategies of War
    d. 28-hour day

4. _____ is a term that has been used in various psychology theories, often in slightly different ways (e.g., Goldstein, Maslow, Rogers.) The term was originally introduced by the organismic theorist Kurt Goldstein for the motive to realise all of one's potentialities. In his view, it is the master motive--indeed, the only real motive a person has, all others being merely manifestations of it.
   a. 33 Strategies of War
   b. 1990 Clean Air Act
   c. 28-hour day
   d. Self-actualization

5. _____ are job factors that can cause dissatisfaction if missing but do not necessarily motivate employees if increased.

   _____ have mostly to do with the job environment. These factors are important or notable only when they are lacking.

   a. Work system
   b. Work-at-home scheme
   c. Split shift
   d. Hygiene factors

6. _____ refers to an individual's desire for significant accomplishment, mastering of skills, control, or high standards. The term was introduced by the psychologist, David McClelland.

   _____ is related to the difficulty of tasks people choose to undertake.

   a. Two-factor theory
   b. Need for power
   c. 1990 Clean Air Act
   d. Need for achievement

7. _____ is a term that was popularized by renowned psychologist David McClelland in 1961. However, it should be recognized that McClellend's thinking was strongly influenced by the pioneering work of Henry Murray who first identified underlying psychological human needs and motivational processes (1938.) It was Murray who set out a taxonomy of needs, including Achievement, Power and Affiliation - and placed these in the context of an integrated motivational model.
   a. Need for power
   b. 1990 Clean Air Act
   c. Two-factor theory
   d. Need for Achievement

Chapter 14. Motivating Organizational Members

8. The _____ is a term that was popularised by David McClelland and describes a person's need to feel a sense of involvement and 'belonging' within a social group. However, it should be recognised that McClellend's thinking was strongly influenced by the pioneering work of Henry Murray who first identified underlying psychological human needs and motivational processes (1938.) It was Murray who set out a taxonomy of needs, including Achievement, Power and Affiliation - and placed these in the context of an integrated motivational model.

   a. Strong-Campbell Interest Inventory
   b. Need for affiliation
   c. SESAMO
   d. Polynomial conjoint measurement

9. _____ attempts to explain relational satisfaction in terms of perceptions of fair/unfair distributions of resources within interpersonal relationships. _____ is considered as one of the justice theories, It was first developed in 1962 by John Stacey Adams, a workplace and behavioral psychologist, who asserted that employees seek to maintain equity between the inputs that they bring to a job and the outcomes that they receive from it against the perceived inputs and outcomes of others (Adams, 1965.) The belief is that people value fair treatment which causes them to be motivated to keep the fairness maintained within the relationships of their co-workers and the organization.

   a. A Stake in the Outcome
   b. Equity theory
   c. AAAI
   d. A4e

10. _____ involves establishing specific, measurable and time-targeted objectives. Work on the theory of goal-setting suggests that it's an effective tool for making progress by ensuring that participants in a group with a common goal are clearly aware of what is expected from them if an objective is to be achieved. On a personal level, setting goals is a process that allows people to specify then work towards their own objectives - most commonly with financial or career-based goals.

    a. Digital strategy
    b. Resource-based view
    c. Goal setting
    d. Catfish effect

11. _____ is the use of empirically demonstrated behavior change techniques to improve behavior, such as altering an individual's behaviors and reactions to stimuli through positive and negative reinforcement of adaptive behavior and/or the reduction of maladaptive behavior through punishment and/or therapy.

The first use of the term _____ appears to have been by Edward Thorndike in 1911

a. 1990 Clean Air Act
b. Behavior modification
c. 33 Strategies of War
d. 28-hour day

12.   In neuroscience, the _____ is a collection of brain structures which attempts to regulate and control behavior by inducing pleasurable effects.

A psychological reward is a process that reinforces behavior -- something that, when offered, causes a behavior to increase in intensity. Reward is an operational concept for describing the positive value an individual ascribes to an object, behavioral act or an internal physical state.

a. 28-hour day
b. 1990 Clean Air Act
c. 33 Strategies of War
d. Reward system

Chapter 15. Organizational Control in a Complex Business Environment

1. _____ is one of the managerial functions like planning, organizing, staffing and directing. It is an important function because it helps to check the errors and to take the corrective action so that deviation from standards are minimized and stated goals of the organization are achieved in desired manner. According to modern concepts, _____ is a foreseeing action whereas earlier concept of _____ was used only when errors were detected. _____ in management means setting standards, measuring actual performance and taking corrective action.

   a. Turnover
   b. Decision tree pruning
   c. Schedule of reinforcement
   d. Control

2. _____ describes the situation when output from (or information about the result of) an event or phenomenon in the past will influence the same event/phenomenon in the present or future. When an event is part of a chain of cause-and-effect that forms a circuit or loop, then the event is said to 'feed back' into itself.

   _____ is also a synonym for:

   - _____ signal; the information about the initial event that is the basis for subsequent modification of the event.
   - _____ loop; the causal path that leads from the initial generation of the _____ signal to the subsequent modification of the event.

   _____ is a mechanism, process or signal that is looped back to control a system within itself. Such a loop is called a _____ loop.

   a. Feedback
   b. 1990 Clean Air Act
   c. Feedback loop
   d. Positive feedback

3. _____ is a 'policy by which management devotes its time to investigating only those situations in which actual results differ significantly from planned results. The idea is that management should spend its valuable time concentrating on the more important items (such as shaping the company's future strategic course.) Attention is given only to material deviations requiring investigation.'

   It is not entirely synonymous with the concept of exception management in that it describes a policy where absolute focus is on exception management, in contrast to moderate application of exception management.

   a. C-A-K-E
   b. Business philosophy
   c. Management by exception
   d. Trustee

Chapter 15. Organizational Control in a Complex Business Environment

4. The 'business case for _____', theorizes that in a global marketplace, a company that employs a diverse workforce (both men and women, people of many generations, people from ethnically and racially diverse backgrounds etc.) is better able to understand the demographics of the marketplace it serves and is thus better equipped to thrive in that marketplace than a company that has a more limited range of employee demographics.

An additional corollary suggests that a company that supports the _____ of its workforce can also improve employee satisfaction, productivity and retention.

   a. Kanban
   b. Diversity
   c. Virtual team
   d. Trademark

5. In economics, business, retail, and accounting, a _____ is the value of money that has been used up to produce something, and hence is not available for use anymore. In economics, a _____ is an alternative that is given up as a result of a decision. In business, the _____ may be one of acquisition, in which case the amount of money expended to acquire it is counted as _____.
   a. Cost
   b. Cost overrun
   c. Cost allocation
   d. Fixed costs

6. _____ are formal records of the financial activities of a business, person, or other entity. In British English, including United Kingdom company law, _____ are often referred to as accounts, although the term _____ is also used, particularly by accountants.

_____ provide an overview of a business or person's financial condition in both short and long term.

   a. 33 Strategies of War
   b. Financial statements
   c. 1990 Clean Air Act
   d. 28-hour day

7. In business and accounting, _____s are everything of value that is owned by a person or company. Any property or object of value that one possesses, usually considered as applicable to the payment of one's debts is considered an _____. Simplistically stated, _____s are things of value that can be readily converted into cash.

Chapter 15. Organizational Control in a Complex Business Environment

a. Asset
b. A Stake in the Outcome
c. A4e
d. AAAI

8. In financial accounting, a _____ or statement of financial position is a summary of a person's or organization's balances. Assets, liabilities and ownership equity are listed as of a specific date, such as the end of its financial year. A _____ is often described as a snapshot of a company's financial condition.
   a. 1990 Clean Air Act
   b. 28-hour day
   c. Balance sheet
   d. 33 Strategies of War

9. In finance, a _____ or accounting ratio is a ratio of two selected numerical values taken from an enterprise's financial statements. There are many standard ratios used to try to evaluate the overall financial condition of a corporation or other organization. _____s may be used by managers within a firm, by current and potential shareholders (owners) of a firm, and by a firm's creditors.
   a. Return on equity
   b. Return on sales
   c. Rate of return
   d. Financial ratio

10. _____ plant, and equipment, is a term used in accountancy for assets and property which cannot easily be converted into cash. This can be compared with current assets such as cash or bank accounts, which are described as liquid assets. In most cases, only tangible assets are referred to as fixed.
    a. 28-hour day
    b. Fixed asset
    c. 33 Strategies of War
    d. 1990 Clean Air Act

11. _____ is a company's financial statement that indicates how the revenue is transformed into the net income The purpose of the _____ is to show managers and investors whether the company made or lost money during the period being reported.

The important thing to remember about an _____ is that it represents a period of time.

Chapter 15. Organizational Control in a Complex Business Environment

a. AAAI
b. A Stake in the Outcome
c. A4e
d. Income statement

12. _____ is a financial ratio that indicates the percentage of a company's assets are provided via debt. It is the ratio of total debt (the sum of current liabilities and long-term liabilities) and total assets (the sum of current assets, fixed assets, and other assets such as 'goodwill'.)

$$\text{Debt ratio} = \frac{\text{Total Debt}}{\text{Total Assets}}$$

or alternatively:

$$\text{Debt ratio} = \frac{\text{Total Liability}}{\text{Total Assets}}$$

For example, a company with $2 million in total assets and $500,000 in total liabilities would have a _____ of 25%

Like all financial ratios, a company's _____ should be compared with their industry average or other competing firms.

a. Debt ratio
b. Demand forecasting
c. 1990 Clean Air Act
d. 28-hour day

13. Market _____ is a business, economics or investment term that refers to an asset's ability to be easily converted through an act of buying or selling without causing a significant movement in the price and with minimum loss of value. Money, or cash on hand, is the most liquid asset. An act of exchange of a less liquid asset with a more liquid asset is called liquidation.

a. 1990 Clean Air Act
b. Liquidity
c. 33 Strategies of War
d. 28-hour day

14. The _____ is the labour pool in employment. It is generally used to describe those working for a single company or industry, but can also apply to a geographic region like a city, country, state, etc. The term generally excludes the employers or management, and implies those involved in manual labour.
   a. Pink-collar worker
   b. Workforce
   c. Division of labour
   d. Work-life balance

Chapter 16. Productivity and Quality in Operations

1. _____ is an area of business concerned with the production of goods and services, and involves the responsibility of ensuring that business operations are efficient in terms of using as little resource as needed, and effective in terms of meeting customer requirements. It is concerned with managing the process that converts inputs (in the forms of materials, labour and energy) into outputs (in the form of goods and services.)

Operations traditionally refers to the production of goods and services separately, although the distinction between these two main types of operations is increasingly difficult to make as manufacturers tend to merge product and service offerings.

    a. Operations management
    b. A4e
    c. A Stake in the Outcome
    d. AAAI

2. _____ is an advertisement in which a particular product specifically mentions a competitor by name for the express purpose of showing why the competitor is inferior to the product naming it.

This should not be confused with parody advertisements, where a fictional product is being advertised for the purpose of poking fun at the particular advertisement, nor should it be confused with the use of a coined brand name for the purpose of comparing the product without actually naming an actual competitor. ('Wikipedia tastes better and is less filling than the Encyclopedia Galactica.')

In the 1980s, during what has been referred to as the cola wars, soft-drink manufacturer Pepsi ran a series of advertisements where people, caught on hidden camera, in a blind taste test, chose Pepsi over rival Coca-Cola.

    a. 1990 Clean Air Act
    b. 28-hour day
    c. 33 Strategies of War
    d. Comparative advertising

3. _____ refers to the movement of cash into or out of a business or financial product. It is usually measured during a specified, finite period of time. Measurement of _____ can be used

- to determine a project's rate of return or value. The time of _____s into and out of projects are used as inputs in financial models such as internal rate of return, and net present value.
- to determine problems with a business's liquidity. Being profitable does not necessarily mean being liquid. A company can fail because of a shortage of cash, even while profitable.
- as an alternate measure of a business's profits when it is believed that accrual accounting concepts do not represent economic realities. For example, a company may be notionally profitable but generating little operational cash (as may be the case for a company that barters its products rather than selling for cash.) In such a case, the company may be deriving additional operating cash by issuing shares evaluating default risk, re-investment requirements, etc.

Chapter 16. Productivity and Quality in Operations

_____ is a generic term used differently depending on the context. It may be defined by users for their own purposes.

a. Sweat equity
b. Gross profit
c. Gross profit margin
d. Cash flow

4. A _____ is a computer program typically used to provide some form of artificial intelligence, which consists primarily of a set of rules about behavior. These rules, termed productions, are a basic representation found useful in AI planning, expert systems and action selection. A _____ provides the mechanism necessary to execute productions in order to achieve some goal for the system.
   a. 33 Strategies of War
   b. 28-hour day
   c. 1990 Clean Air Act
   d. Production system

5. _____ can be defined as the idea generation, concept development, testing and manufacturing or implementation of a physical object or service. _____ers conceptualize and evaluate ideas, making them tangible through products in a more systematic approach. The role of a _____er encompasses many characteristics of the marketing manager, product manager, industrial designer and design engineer.
   a. Adam Smith
   b. Affiliation
   c. Abraham Harold Maslow
   d. Product design

6. _____ is a branch of operations research concerning itself with mathematical modeling and solution of problems concerning the placement of facilities in order to minimize transportation costs, avoid placing hazardous materials near housing, outperform competitors' facilities, etc.

A simple _____ problem is the Fermat-Weber problem, in which a single facility is to be placed, with the only optimization criterion being the minimization of the sum of distances from a given set of point sites. More complex problems considered in this discipline include the placement of multiple facilities, constraints on the locations of facilities, and more complex optimization criteria.

a. 1990 Clean Air Act
b. Facility location
c. 28-hour day
d. Multiscale decision making

7. _____ is an operational activity which does an aggregate plan for the production process, in advance of 2 to 18 months, to give an idea to management as to what quantity of materials and other resources are to be procured and when, so that the total cost of operations of the organization is kept to the minimum over that period.

The quantity of outsourcing, subcontracting of items, overtime of labor, numbers to be hired and fired in each period and the amount of inventory to be held in stock and to be backlogged for each period are decided. All of these activities are done within the framework of the company ethics, policies, and long term commitment to the society, community and the country of operation.

a. Aggregate planning
b. A Stake in the Outcome
c. Earned Schedule
d. Earned value management

8. A _____ is a plan for production, staffing, inventory, etc. It is usually linked to manufacturing where the plan indicates when and how much of each product will be demanded. This plan quantifies significant processes, parts, and other resources in order to optimize production, to identify bottlenecks, and to anticipate needs and completed goods.

a. Remanufacturing
b. Value engineering
c. Piecework
d. Master production schedule

9. _____ is the level of inventory that minimizes the total inventory holding costs and ordering costs. The framework used to determine this order quantity is also known as Wilson _____ Model. The model was developed by F. W. Harris in 1913.

a. Economic order quantity
b. Event management
c. Effective executive
d. Anti-leadership

Chapter 16. Productivity and Quality in Operations

10. _____ is an inventory strategy that strives to improve the return on investment of a business by reducing in-process inventory and its associated carrying costs. To meet _____ objectives, the process relies on signals between different points in the process. This means the process is often driven by a series of signals, or Kanban, which tell production when to make the next part. Kanban are usually 'tickets' but can be simple visual signals, such as the presence or absence of a part on a shelf. Implemented correctly, _____ can dramatically improve a manufacturing organization's return on investment, quality, and efficiency.

   a. 28-hour day
   b. 33 Strategies of War
   c. 1990 Clean Air Act
   d. Just-in-time

11. A _____ is the system of organizations, people, technology, activities, information and resources involved in moving a product or service from supplier to customer. _____ activities transform natural resources, raw materials and components into a finished product that is delivered to the end customer. In sophisticated _____ systems, used products may re-enter the _____ at any point where residual value is recyclable.

   a. Wholesalers
   b. Drop shipping
   c. Packaging
   d. Supply chain

12. _____ refers to metrics and measures of output from production processes, per unit of input. Labor _____, for example, is typically measured as a ratio of output per labor-hour, an input. _____ may be conceived of as a metrics of the technical or engineering efficiency of production.

   a. Value engineering
   b. Remanufacturing
   c. Master production schedule
   d. Productivity

13. In engineering and manufacturing, _____ and quality engineering are used in developing systems to ensure products or services are designed and produced to meet or exceed customer requirements. Refer to the definition by Merriam-Webster for further information. These systems are often developed in conjunction with other business and engineering disciplines using a cross-functional approach.

   a. Statistical process control
   b. Quality control
   c. Process capability
   d. Single Minute Exchange of Die

Chapter 16. Productivity and Quality in Operations

14. _____ is one of the managerial functions like planning, organizing, staffing and directing. It is an important function because it helps to check the errors and to take the corrective action so that deviation from standards are minimized and stated goals of the organization are achieved in desired manner. According to modern concepts, _____ is a foreseeing action whereas earlier concept of _____ was used only when errors were detected. _____ in management means setting standards, measuring actual performance and taking corrective action.

   a. Turnover
   b. Schedule of reinforcement
   c. Decision tree pruning
   d. Control

15. _____ refers to planned and systematic production processes that provide confidence in a product's suitability for its intended purpose. Refer to the definition by Merriam-Webster for further information. It is a set of activities intended to ensure that products (goods and/or services) satisfy customer requirements in a systematic, reliable fashion.

   a. 28-hour day
   b. Quality assurance
   c. Risk assessment
   d. 1990 Clean Air Act

16. _____ is a business management strategy aimed at embedding awareness of quality in all organizational processes. _____ has been widely used in manufacturing, education, hospitals, call centers, government, and service industries, as well as NASA space and science programs.

   As defined by the International Organization for Standardization (ISO):

   '_____ is a management approach for an organization, centered on quality, based on the participation of all its members and aiming at long-term success through customer satisfaction, and benefits to all members of the organization and to society.' ISO 8402:1994

   One major aim is to reduce variation from every process so that greater consistency of effort is obtained. (Royse, D., Thyer, B., Padgett D., ' Logan T., 2006)

   a. 1990 Clean Air Act
   b. Total quality management
   c. Quality management
   d. 28-hour day

17. In economics, business, retail, and accounting, a _____ is the value of money that has been used up to produce something, and hence is not available for use anymore. In economics, a _____ is an alternative that is given up as a result of a decision. In business, the _____ may be one of acquisition, in which case the amount of money expended to acquire it is counted as _____.

Chapter 16. Productivity and Quality in Operations

77

a. Cost
b. Cost allocation
c. Fixed costs
d. Cost overrun

18. The concept of quality costs is a means to quantify the total _____-related efforts and deficiencies. It was first described by Armand V. Feigenbaum in a 1956 Harvard Business Review article.

Prior to its introduction, the general perception was that higher quality requires higher costs, either by buying better materials or machines or by hiring more labor.

a. Cost of Quality
b. Quality costs
c. Fixed costs
d. Cost accounting

19. _____ can be considered to have three main components: quality control, quality assurance and quality improvement. _____ is focused not only on product quality, but also the means to achieve it. _____ therefore uses quality assurance and control of processes as well as products to achieve more consistent quality.

a. Total quality management
b. 1990 Clean Air Act
c. 28-hour day
d. Quality management

20. _____ is the process of comparing the cost, cycle time, productivity, or quality of a specific process or method to another that is widely considered to be an industry standard or best practice. Essentially, _____ provides a snapshot of the performance of your business and helps you understand where you are in relation to a particular standard. The result is often a business case for making changes in order to make improvements.

a. Benchmarking
b. Cost leadership
c. Complementors
d. Competitive heterogeneity

21. _____ is a technical term used in management science popularized by Joseph M. Juran

He defined an internal and external customers as anyone affected by the product or by the process used to produce the product, in the context of quality management. _____s may play the role as supplier, processor, and customer in the sequence of product development.

Chapter 16. Productivity and Quality in Operations

He claimed that the organization must understand and identify both internal and external customers and their needs.

a. A Stake in the Outcome
b. Internal customer
c. AAAI
d. A4e

22. _____ is a concept related to the relative abilities of parties in a situation to exert influence over each other. If both parties are on an equal footing in a debate, then they will have equal _____, such as in a perfectly competitive market, or between an evenly matched monopoly and monopsony.

There are a number of fields where the concept of _____ has proven crucial to coherent analysis: game theory, labour economics, collective bargaining arrangements, diplomatic negotiations, settlement of litigation, the price of insurance, and any negotiation in general.

a. Trade credit
b. 1990 Clean Air Act
c. Bargaining power
d. Buy-sell agreement

23. _____ is a Japanese philosophy that focuses on continuous improvement throughout all aspects of life. When applied to the workplace, _____ activities continually improve all functions of a business, from manufacturing to management and from the CEO to the assembly line workers. By improving standardized activities and processes, _____ aims to eliminate waste .

a. Sensitivity analysis
b. Kaizen
c. Psychological pricing
d. Cross-docking

24. A _____ is a volunteer group composed of workers (or even students), usually under the leadership of their supervisor (but they can elect a team leader), who are trained to identify, analyse and solve work-related problems and present their solutions to management in order to improve the performance of the organization, and motivate and enrich the work of employees. When matured, true _____s become self-managing, having gained the confidence of management.
_____s are an alternative to the dehumanising concept of the Division of Labour, where workers or individuals are treated like robots.

a. Certified in Production and Inventory Management
b. Connectionist expert systems
c. Competency-based job descriptions
d. Quality circle

25. _____ is a company-wide computer software system used to manage and coordinate all the resources, information, and functions of a business from shared data stores.

An _____ system has a service-oriented architecture with modular hardware and software units and 'services' that communicate on a local area network. The modular design allows a business to add or reconfigure modules (perhaps from different vendors) while preserving data integrity in one shared database that may be centralized or distributed.

a. A Stake in the Outcome
b. A4e
c. AAAI
d. Enterprise resource planning

Chapter 17. Information Technology and Control

1. _____ in its literal sense is the process of transformation of local or regional phenomena into global ones. It can be described as a process by which the people of the world are unified into a single society and function together.

This process is a combination of economic, technological, sociocultural and political forces.

   a. Collaborative Planning, Forecasting and Replenishment
   b. Histogram
   c. Cost Management
   d. Globalization

2. An _____ is a mostly hierarchical concept of subordination of entities that collaborate and contribute to serve one common aim.

Organizations are a variant of clustered entities. The structure of an organization is usually set up in many a styles, dependent on their objectives and ambience.

   a. Informal organization
   b. Organizational structure
   c. Open shop
   d. Organizational development

3. _____, e-commuting, e-work, telework, working from home (WFH), or working at home (WAH) is a work arrangement in which employees enjoy flexibility in working location and hours. In other words, the daily commute to a central place of work is replaced by telecommunication links. Many work from home, while others, occasionally also referred to as nomad workers or web commuters utilize mobile telecommunications technology to work from coffee shops or myriad other locations.
   a. 33 Strategies of War
   b. 1990 Clean Air Act
   c. 28-hour day
   d. Telecommuting

4. _____, commonly known as e-commerce, consists of the buying and selling of products or services over electronic systems such as the Internet and other computer networks. The amount of trade conducted electronically has grown extraordinarily with widespread Internet usage. The use of commerce is conducted in this way, spurring and drawing on innovations in electronic funds transfer, supply chain management, Internet marketing, online transaction processing, electronic data interchange (EDI), inventory management systems, and automated data collection systems.

Chapter 17. Information Technology and Control

a. Electronic Commerce
b. A Stake in the Outcome
c. A4e
d. Online shopping

5. _____ constitute a class of computer-based information systems including knowledge-based systems that support decision-making activities.

_____ are a specific class of computerized information systems that supports business and organizational decision-making activities. A properly-designed _____ is an interactive software-based system intended to help decision makers compile useful information from raw data, documents, personal knowledge, and/or business models to identify and solve problems and make decisions.

a. Decision support systems
b. 28-hour day
c. 1990 Clean Air Act
d. Spatial Decision Support Systems

6. _____ is a company-wide computer software system used to manage and coordinate all the resources, information, and functions of a business from shared data stores.

An _____ system has a service-oriented architecture with modular hardware and software units and 'services' that communicate on a local area network. The modular design allows a business to add or reconfigure modules (perhaps from different vendors) while preserving data integrity in one shared database that may be centralized or distributed.

a. AAAI
b. A4e
c. Enterprise resource planning
d. A Stake in the Outcome

7. _____ comprises a range of practices used in an organisation to identify, create, represent, distribute and enable adoption of insights and experiences. Such insights and experiences comprise knowledge, either embodied in individuals or embedded in organisational processes or practice.

An established discipline since 1991, _____ includes courses taught in the fields of business administration, information systems, management, and library and information sciences.

Chapter 17. Information Technology and Control

a. 1990 Clean Air Act
b. 28-hour day
c. 33 Strategies of War
d. Knowledge management

8. _____ refers to a (generally IT based) system for managing knowledge in organizations for supporting creation, capture, storage and dissemination of information. It can comprise a part (neither necessary or sufficient) of a Knowledge Management initiative.

The idea of a _____ is to enable employees to have ready access to the organization's documented base of facts, sources of information, and solutions.

a. 33 Strategies of War
b. Knowledge management system
c. 1990 Clean Air Act
d. 28-hour day

9. _____ is the use of control systems (such as numerical control, programmable logic control, and other industrial control systems), in concert with other applications of information technology (such as computer-aided technologies [CAD, CAM, CAx]), to control industrial machinery and processes, reducing the need for human intervention. In the scope of industrialization, _____ is a step beyond mechanization. Whereas mechanization provided human operators with machinery to assist them with the physical requirements of work, _____ greatly reduces the need for human sensory and mental requirements as well.

a. A4e
b. AAAI
c. A Stake in the Outcome
d. Automation

10. _____ is the use of an object (typically referred to as an RFID tag) applied to or incorporated into a product, animal, or person for the purpose of identification and tracking using radio waves. Some tags can be read from several meters away and beyond the line of sight of the reader.

Most RFID tags contain at least two parts.

a. 1990 Clean Air Act
b. Radio-frequency identification
c. 33 Strategies of War
d. 28-hour day

11. _____ refers to the structured transmission of data between organizations by electronic means. It is used to transfer electronic documents from one computer system to another (ie) from one trading partner to another trading partner. It is more than mere E-mail; for instance, organizations might replace bills of lading and even checks with appropriate _____ messages.
   a. A Stake in the Outcome
   b. Electronic data interchange
   c. AAAI
   d. A4e

12. _____ is the intelligence of machines and the branch of computer science which aims to create it. Major _____ textbooks define the field as 'the study and design of intelligent agents,' where an intelligent agent is a system that perceives its environment and takes actions which maximize its chances of success. John McCarthy, who coined the term in 1956, defines it as 'the science and engineering of making intelligent machines.'

The field was founded on the claim that a central property of human beings, intelligence--the sapience of Homo sapiens--can be so precisely described that it can be simulated by a machine.

   a. A4e
   b. AAAI
   c. A Stake in the Outcome
   d. Artificial intelligence

13. An _____ is software that attempts to reproduce the performance of one or more human experts, most commonly in a specific problem domain, and is a traditional application and/or subfield of artificial intelligence. A wide variety of methods can be used to simulate the performance of the expert however common to most or all are 1) the creation of a so-called 'knowledgebase' which uses some knowledge representation formalism to capture the Subject Matter Experts (SME) knowledge and 2) a process of gathering that knowledge from the SME and codifying it according to the formalism, which is called knowledge engineering. _____s may or may not have learning components but a third common element is that once the system is developed it is proven by being placed in the same real world problem solving situation as the human SME, typically as an aid to human workers or a supplement to some information system.
   a. A Stake in the Outcome
   b. A4e
   c. AAAI
   d. Expert system

ANSWER KEY

Chapter 1
1. c   2. a   3. d   4. b   5. d   6. a   7. d   8. d   9. c   10. d
11. d   12. c   13. a   14. d   15. d   16. d   17. d

Chapter 2
1. c   2. d   3. a   4. c   5. d   6. c   7. a   8. d   9. d   10. a
11. b   12. b   13. d   14. a   15. a   16. a   17. d   18. c   19. d   20. b

Chapter 3
1. b   2. c   3. b   4. d   5. b   6. d   7. a   8. b   9. d   10. d
11. d   12. d

Chapter 4
1. b   2. a   3. d   4. d   5. c   6. d   7. a   8. d   9. b   10. d
11. d   12. d   13. d   14. b   15. c   16. d   17. a   18. d   19. a

Chapter 5
1. d   2. d   3. d   4. d   5. b   6. d   7. a   8. d   9. c   10. c
11. d   12. c   13. d   14. d   15. d   16. b   17. b   18. c

Chapter 6
1. b   2. d   3. b   4. d   5. b   6. d   7. d   8. c   9. b   10. d
11. d   12. d   13. a   14. a   15. d   16. a   17. b   18. d

Chapter 7
1. d   2. d   3. d   4. c   5. a   6. d   7. d   8. a   9. a   10. d
11. d   12. d   13. c   14. c

Chapter 8
1. d   2. c   3. a   4. b   5. d   6. d   7. d

Chapter 9
1. c   2. b   3. a   4. b   5. d   6. b   7. b   8. d   9. d   10. d
11. b   12. a   13. b   14. d   15. c   16. c   17. b   18. c   19. c   20. d
21. d   22. c   23. b   24. d   25. b   26. d   27. b   28. d   29. b   30. d

Chapter 10
1. a   2. d   3. b

Chapter 11
1. a   2. d   3. c

Chapter 12
1. b   2. a   3. d   4. b   5. d   6. b   7. d   8. d

ANSWER KEY

Chapter 13
1. d   2. a   3. c   4. c   5. d   6. d   7. d   8. c   9. b   10. d
11. c 12. c 13. a 14. c 15. d

Chapter 14
1. a   2. c   3. a   4. d   5. d   6. d   7. a   8. b   9. b   10. c
11. b 12. d

Chapter 15
1. d   2. a   3. c   4. b   5. a   6. b   7. a   8. c   9. d   10. b
11. d 12. a 13. b 14. b

Chapter 16
1. a   2. d   3. d   4. d   5. d   6. b   7. a   8. d   9. a   10. d
11. d 12. d 13. b 14. d 15. b 16. b 17. a 18. a 19. d 20. a
21. b 22. c 23. b 24. d 25. d

Chapter 17
1. d   2. b   3. d   4. a   5. a   6. c   7. d   8. b   9. d   10. b
11. b 12. d 13. d

www.ingramcontent.com/pod-product-compliance
Lightning Source LLC
Chambersburg PA
CBHW081848230426
43669CB00018B/2867